Alaska Gold Trail

Volume IV

The Life of And The Life of
Felix Pedro Earl Pilgrim

Presented By
Jim Madonna

Life in Alaska's Frontier
as Told by the Pioneers Who Blazed the Trails

Cover Photo:
Felix Pedro with discovery claim on Pedro Creek located north of Fairbanks, Alaska shown in the background.

Pedro image courtesy of University of Alaska Archives.

ISBN: 1-891733-19-2
All rights reserved
© 2006 by James A. Madonna

Published by A.P. Publishing
Fairbanks, Alaska

Dedicated to
Leah

Acknowledgment

This book was made possible only through the cooperation of friends deeply interested in this period of Alaska's history. Their condensed biographies are included, along with the lives of Felix Pedro and Earl Pilgrim. Without their contributions this volume could not have been written. I would like to extend my special gratitude to these people.

Always urging me to go on were two people: my wife, Leah, who, when my progress began to slow to that of a snail, urged me to pick up the pace. And my long time friend Sharon Kessey, who over the past few years has been asking me what the holdup was. I am grateful for her gentle push, but also for her eager enthusiasm and support in critically reading and editing this manuscript. Since the beginning of the Alaska Gold Trail series, Leah and Sharon have always stood in the background waiting to come forward and do their part in making these four volumes a reality. It is said with genuine sincerity, that I am forever indebted to them.

Table Of Contents

Dedication..iii

Acknowledgment...iv

Figure: Alaska Communities and Trails of the Pioneers........vi

Part I: Introduction...1

Part II: Previews from Volume IV.......................................3

Part III: Felix Pedro...7

JohneBinkley...8

Terrence Cole...32

Shann Jones...37

Massimo Turchi..57

The Life of Felix Pedro...59

Part IV: Earl Pilgrim...121

Jim Lounsbury...122

Leah Madonna..136

The Life of Earl Pilgrim..147

Part V: Where the Trail Winds..173

Part VI: Appendices and Suggested Reading.......................177

Appendix I: Alaska Facts...178

Appendix II: Alaska Gold Discoveries..................................179

Appendix III: Suggested Reading..181

Pioneers Featured in Volumes I, II and III.............................183

Figure : Alaska Communities and Trails of Pioneers

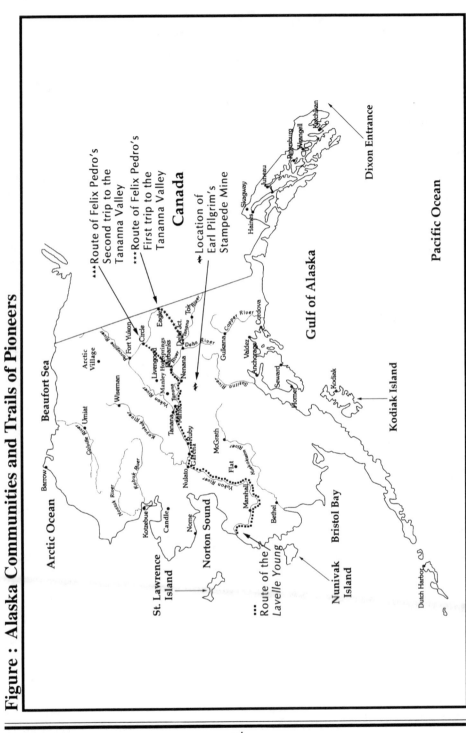

Part I
Introduction

The trail is never straight. We all make decisions which alter the direction our life will take. You do it, I do it, and for certain the many pioneers presented in the four volumes of Alaska Gold Trails did it. Not all of these decisions are earth-shattering life changes. Some are subtle, and yet they send us off into new worlds that we have not before tested. And when you think about it, it is the mystery of the future that creates the adventure.

****

I would like to share one of my small deviations from the trail with you. Volumes I, II, and III of Alaska Gold Trails were drawn largely from interviews with Alaskan Pioneers during KFAR radio shows held in the late 1980s. Volumes I and II had been published and I was well into Volume III when, in the winter of 2001, I became infatuated with the life of one of Alaska's most famous pioneers, Felix Pedro. He was the Italian immigrant who first discovered gold in the Tanana Valley and was one of the men who was instrumental in the birth and development of Fairbanks, Alaska. In the spring of 2001 my longtime friend Tim Sander and I took a fact-finding trip to Fanano, Italy, to visit Felix's birthplace and burial site. With the help of Fanano's head of tourism, Massimo Turchi, we gathered a rich background covering Felix's youth up until his departure to the United States. For the following year I continued to research Felix's life. Many surprises surfaced as the results of his adventurous lifestyle unfolded. In July of 2002 I was honored to give the centenial presentation of the first gold discovery in Fairbanks, Alaska, and a summary of Felix's life to a large gathering from across the United States and a large group of Italian relatives and friends who visited from Fanano, Italy. What an enjoyable and memorable event it was.

One may ask what was the deviation? The answer is that I was in the middle of editing Volume III of Alaska Gold Trails. And while I didn't exactly set it aside, progress did slow to a snail's pace.

Some asked what drew me to Felix Pedro. A suggestion could be that I was tightly involved with the Alaskan gold mining industry during the 26 years I taught the Mining Extension courses at the University of Alaska, and to fully understand the industry one should be aware of its history. A lot of it had to do with these two possibilities, but even more, the magnetism was Felix's passion for life and adventurous soul. This is a story that needed to be told.

It is with great pleasure that I join with my friends Johne Binkley, Terrence Cole, Shann Jones and Massimo Turchi to present **The Life of Felix Pedro**.

****

About this same period of time (2002) an additional turn in the trail occurred; I was reminded of a taped interview conducted by my wife, Leah Madonna, and Jim Lounsbury, of another famous Alaskan Pioneer, Earl Pilgrim. It was a sterling presentation filled with exciting anecdotes of life in Alaska, and was shouting to be presented. As a result I decided to include Earl's life in this volume.

There were a couple of different elements that drew me to Earl besides his actual mining history. He was known to be a feisty little fellow, some referred to it as athletically aggressive. I call it openly spirited. Perhaps what drew me to Earl was not only the fact that we were both athletic and fashioned from the same spirited mold, but the fact that we had one other very interesting link. Earl Pilgrim taught the very first mining short course at the University of Alaska—according to his memory in 1924—and I am sorry to say that I taught the very last mining short course at the University of Alaska in 1999. I will be eternally saddened that the Mining Extension program did not continue following my retirement. Sorry Earl.

For the past three years all my spare writing time has been taken up with preparing the edited manuscript from the tape presented by this colorful pioneer. I am privileged to join with Leah Madonna and Jim Lounsbury to present **The Life of Earl Pilgrim.**

****

So you see how the path that featured predominantly pioneers interviewed on a radio show has deviated into presentations covering the lives of pioneers who never heard of, or would ever know of, Alaska Gold Trails. It was a good turn in the trail, and from my perspective it was time well spent. Hope you enjoy these presentations as much as I have enjoyed presenting them.

Jim Madonna

Part II

Previews

There are always challenges we dream of facing in our lives, but for some reason known only to us personally, we never quite get around to them. Time alone dictates that we cannot be or do all things in this short time we have on Earth. Fortunately, those of us interested in the rugged outdoor adventure associated with Alaska's vast wilderness can live some of our dreams through the lives and experiences of the early frontiersmen and settling pioneers. As you read these accounts of their colorful frontier lives and the obstacles they faced during the time they blazed the trail into the country, just possibly, one of their experiences will stir your restless spirit and spark an unresistable challenge that forces you to take the first step down the trail to that one last big frontier adventure—towards the fulfillment of your destiny.

Felix Pedro: "In the year 1895 I went to Alaska and stopped at Forty Mile on the Yukon River and commenced mining and prospecting and continued so to do off and on until the year 1899; that about that time I came down to Circle City and went out prospecting and continued so doing until 1902 when I made a strike on what is known as Pedro Creek."

Johne Binkley: When Johne was asked how he liked the years he spent running riverboats in Western Alaska he replied, "Oh, I loved it! It was just tremendous. You know, just a lot of those same memories of stories my father would tell me about getting stuck on river sandbars and how they would get off. Those were the same things that I lived during those ten years. Watching those beautiful sunrises and sunsets while I was up there alone in the wheelhouse. It is so peaceful and beautiful at three o'clock in the morning, running up there on the river when the sun is just coming up. It was great, and working with the native people in the villages up and down the river was just wonderful."

Terrence Cole: When asked how he decided to write about E. T. Barnette, Terrence replied, "My original idea was to use the Tanana Valley Railroad as the vehicle for telling the story of the history of Fairbanks and the surrounding mining camps. Then I realized that a better vehicle might be E.T. Barnette himself because there was not really much known about him, and so much of it was very contradictory. I still remember a picture that Frank Young believed was E.T. Barnette, and I thought,

'Geez, I don't think that's who that is.' There was very little written about Barnette at that time. Bill Cashen had written a very nice, sort of brief treatment of the history of Fairbanks, and had noted that everybody in Fairbanks always said that Barnette was convicted of embezzling money from his bank when it went broke and then skipped town. I thought, 'Well, this is an interesting thing. So, what happened to this guy?' Like I said, there was this debate over who was in this picture, and Frank said it was this one guy. Other people said it was other people. This famous picture of the bankers of Fairbanks—they're all lined up behind a big shipment of gold dust heading Outside from the First National Bank of Fairbanks and Fairbanks Banking Company, which was Barnette's banking company at the time. It's a really great picture, but anyway there's one very shifty-eyed character, and that's who a lot of people were identifying as E.T. Barnette. The more I looked into this mystery about him—maybe not mystery, maybe lack of knowledge—I learned we didn't know how old he was when he was here and we didn't know his exact name. He went by "E.T." Some people said it was Elbridge, some said his name was Ebenezzer. So we didn't know where he was born, didn't know his name. We didn't know what he looked like. We didn't know where he died, and didn't really know hardly anything about this guy at all. So my focus shifted from the railroad to Barnette."

Shann Jones: Shann tells us about one of his more memorable fishing experiences. "Jim and I and his dogs flew into Chandalar Lake in Jim's Cessna 206, took a portable inflatable rubber boat about ten miles up the Chandalar River to the mouth of Baby Creek. There we had set up the tent after we had boated all night. The next morning we could hear wolves howling. Now this was late morning. Jim's smaller dog, Cindy, was looking and barking at something that I thought was across the river. I thought it could be a wolf, and I really didn't want to get involved with that. She kept staring across the river. I was trying to figure out what she was looking at over there, because the brush over there wasn't taller than waist high. Finally, I looked down into the stream, and there was this huge Arctic grayling. That thing was 20 inches plus, as sure as I am sitting here. It was stuck in the low current. Your mantra in the field is 'more food is better.' So I scoop up this fish. I run it over to the tent. I caught it in my bare hand, and it's trying to squirm away. 'Hey, Jim, you want fish for breakfast?'

Massimo Turchi: When asked if he knew any of Felix Pedro's family Massimo replied, "Yes, one of his distant relatives, John Franco Pedroni, knew a lot about Felix. When his father was a young boy he knew Felix and he told John Franco many stories about Felix's adventures in Alaska."

Earl Pilgrim: When asked what the University of Alaska was like when he first arrived to begin teaching, Earl replied, "It was the beginning. The school had not been started yet. I was the first. There were five of us, I think. You know, I was just sick. Not ill but disappointed when I arrived. I had envisioned buildings and all that. When I met and learned to know Judge Bunnell that made it worse. He lived solely to build up his record and compare it to the man that defeated him in election for Alaska Delegate. Right from the start I figured Judge Bunnell was an ex-politician and a windbag—a first-class windbag, and I never changed my mind on that."

Jim Lounsbury: When asked to tell the story about Earl Pilgrim's reaction following the signing of papers for transfer of the Stampede Mine, Jim replied, "Yeah, you were at that big to-do. It was the graduating banquet for the University Mining Engineers and I am trying to think what year that was...early '80s, and this fellow Ed Dole had purchased the property from Earl, and his nephew was there, and they'd just signed the papers. He promised Earl that he would replace some timbers in the adit, and get right after the mine. Soon as he signed the papers, in a loud voice he said, 'There's nothing in the ground. It's worthless.' So he turned it over to the University and later, through D2, somehow the Park Service got involved. Anyway, Earl knew he'd been shafted then." When asked what Earl did at the party Jim said, "Okay, that was a good one. This Ed Dole had the press there with him with their big fancy cameras, and he was running around with his hand sticking straight out trying to catch up with Earl to get this famous promotional picture for what he was going to do, and Earl caught wind of what was going on, and Leah, your wife, was tipped off on it. So she took Earl out on the floor dancing, and they danced for, I'll bet, 45 minutes around that place. They stayed just one step ahead of Ed Dole. It was just a comical thing to see."

Leah Madonna: When asked to tell the story about the night she and Earl Pilgrim danced, she said, "Well first there is some background you should know. First, Earl wasn't a big man. In fact he was not much taller than me and I am 5 feet 2 inches. The second was that Earl first came to Alaska to teach at the University. He left a few years later with a great deal of bitterness toward the college. In short, he was not a friend of the University. The story I am about to tell occurred a few years ago at the Society of Mining Engineers banquet held in the spring of the year. Earl had sold his antimony mine at Stampede to this big company, with the understanding that they were going to mine the ore. Well, the night of the banquet the executive director, I think it was, announced that the company was going to donate that mine to the University of Alaska Fairbanks. Earl, at that time was in his 80s and recognized immediately that the purchase of his mine was nothing more than a write-off by the big company. The announcement infuriated Earl. To calm him down I was asked to go dance with Earl, which I did. We were out on the dance floor, and wouldn't you know it, this executive decided he wanted to dance with his wife. So they entered the dance floor. Well, Earl was still boiling, and as we danced around the floor he maneuvered us over next to this guy and when we got close, Earl took a poke at him."

Part III

Felix Pedro

with

Johne Binkley
Terrence Cole
Shann Jones
Massimo Turchi

and

Jim Madonna

Johne Binkley
with
Jim Madonna
October 26, 2001

Jim: Today our traveling microphone has followed the trail to Riverboat Discovery on the shores of the Chena River in Fairbanks, Alaska, where we are meeting with Johne Binkley. Welcome to Alaska Gold Trails, Johne.

Johne: Thanks for coming over, Jim. I think this will be an interesting meeting and give us both a chance to reminisce a little.

Jim: In the future we are going to discuss the founding of Fairbanks and the life of Felix Pedro, but first, Johne, let's get a little background on you—where you came from, when you were born, and how you happened to become a riverboat captain in Alaska.

Johne: Sure Jim. I was born here in Fairbanks on February 4, 1953, in St. Joseph's Hospital. My wife was born here also. I was born into a riverboating family; my father was a riverboat pilot most all of his life. He was born in Wrangell, Alaska, in 1920, and his father was a riverboat pilot as well. Starting back when my grandfather came up to Alaska during the Klondike Gold Rush, like so many thousands of others who came north, he was a young man looking for adventure and fortune here in the Northland. He came over the Chilkoot Pass, but rather than mining for gold, he started piloting riverboats, initially with rafts, down the upper Yukon, helping a lot of those stampeders get through the perils of the upper Yukon River—Whitehorse Rapids, Miles Canyon and some of those other tough whitewater areas.

Jim: Those were the areas where a lot of people died or lost their outfits trying to get through on their own. He must have been thoroughly familiar with the rapids to pilot all the many types of rafts and boats the early stampeders constructed at the headwaters of the Yukon River to travel the hundreds of miles down to Dawson.

Johne: Yes, he was. That's where he got his start really. He knew riverboating from when he was a young man on the Ohio River, and so he fell naturally into that niche. It wasn't until he teamed up with Sid Berrington, who was another riverboater, that the two of them started working a lot of the smaller streams—the side streams that fed into the Yukon and the Tanana River. These smaller drainages were where they could use smaller boats and establish a certain little niche in the riverboating business of getting miners and prospectors, trappers and traders way up into those more remote areas. So they built smaller, very shallow-draft boats that could navigate some of those small tributaries. They worked all over Alaska, ending up on the Stikine River in Southeast Alaska. At one point they were working out of Anchorage for the Alaska Railroad, which is kind of fascinating for me to think back in history about how my grandfather helped some of the early surveyors working with the Alaska Railroad get their supplies and materials up the Susitna River to do some of the early surveying. I think that was in 1914 and 1915. Then they moved down to Wrangell in Southeast Alaska and started working on the Stikine River hauling miners up to the mining operations near Telegraph. Again, the Stikine is a very shallow, swift river. It comes from Interior B.C. (British Columbia), Canada, and actually transitions into the coast near Wrangell. My grandfather was living in Wrangell, and that's where my father was born. My grandfather died when my dad was very young. His uncle continued to run the business. My father worked with his uncle, learning the business on the Stikine, and then ended up coming up to the University of Alaska here in Fairbanks. He worked his way through college on the riverboats in the summer here in Fairbanks and in the Interior, and then went to school in the wintertime. He really fell in love with the Interior part of Alaska, and was so enamored with running the freight boats up and down the Tanana and Yukon rivers, becoming acquainted with the Athabascan culture (the people of Interior Alaska), and the unending beauty of the river and Alaska, he wanted to share that with others. Another young entrepreneur, Chuck West, was starting his tour business here in Fairbanks. He asked my mother and father if they would take passengers—visitors—out on the river and share some of those experiences. My father jumped at that chance because he really did want an opportunity to share his experiences with others. So, Mom and Dad started the tour business in 1950. It really took all that they had learned and seen around Alaska—the village life, the life of the Athabascans, the trappers, the traders, the missionaries up and down the Yukon—and they condensed that into a four-hour tour out of Fairbanks.

People who didn't have time to get out and actually see the Alaska culture for themselves could get some glimpse of it and experience it in a short period of time as they came through Fairbanks. I was born into that environment, growing up, working with my mother and father and my siblings, sharing with visitors the experiences my father had on the rivers.

Jim: As a young boy, did you entertain visitors on the riverboat tours?

Johne: Well I did it, of course, working on the riverboat. I never did do the commentary.

Jim: You simply interrelated with the passengers?

Johne: Exactly, and we learned that, and those were great skills.

Jim: Those were personal interrelationships rather than as a commentator where you were talking to the entire group of passengers. You were talking one-on-one, is that accurate?

Johne: That's correct, and we learned from a very early age how to interact with older people that were much senior to our young age. It was a great experience, really. In looking back on it, I think a lot of that really helped in forming my personality and my demeanor, and how I relate to people today. I learned a lot of interpersonal skills in dealing with visitors on the riverboat, but I also learned a lot of technical skills because our father was very good about teaching us to handle riverboats and about boating in general. So I learned those skills, as did my brothers. Also, we learned a very critical skill, and that was how to read the water, and how to navigate, particularly on the Tanana, which has its own challenges, as you know, in terms of navigation. We also learned the mechanical aspects of the boats. My father built all of our own equipment. He taught us to weld and cut and fit when we were very young and to basically do everything ourselves, from rebuilding the engine and machinery to maintaining it, to doing some carpentry work, some electrical, plumbing, welding, fitting...you had to do everything. So we learned a lot of those things while growing up as well, all of which have been valuable skills. A great love of mine really is the mechanical side; I really enjoy mechanical things.

Jim: You've got to, don't you? You can't just run the boat; you have to know what makes it run. It is amazing how many times people operate machinery, and all they do is operate machinery. If it ever broke, they wouldn't have a clue what to do or how to fix it.

John: That is right, they wouldn't have a clue. They push the throttle, but they don't know what happens. All they know is that the car goes. They don't know all the things that happen.

Jim: It is important for a person in the type of work that you are in to have all of those types of skills. I have the impression that as a riverboat captain out on the river you must know, without hesitation, what to do in case of a breakdown or emergency.

Johne: That's right.

Jim: Riverbars are tough to get off of.

Johne: Oh yeah! I'm fortunate to have grown up learning those things.

Jim: How many brothers and sisters do you have?

Johne: I have two older brothers and a younger sister. All of us worked in the business.

Jim: Did all of you become riverboat captains?

Johne: My younger sister did not. My two older brothers preceded me in getting their licenses, and I, of course, got my U.S. Coast Guard license as well. We also learned a lot of boating skills. We lived on Noyes Slough when we were growing up. Of course, in those days, we would take the Riverboat Discovery every night right up to our home on Noyes Slough. It was a real river in those days. My father built the boat right there on our property and launched it into Noyes Slough. We built a boat when we were kids—a wooden boat—ourselves, had a little 18-horse-power Evenrude on that wooden boat and we were up and down that slough all the time. That was our transportation. We'd take our bicycles and put them in the boat, then we would take them up the slough, all the way into town of course, or if we were going to baseball practice, we'd take them up Noyes Slough and park the boat in the woods and then get on our bicycles and go to baseball practice. You learn a lot doing those kinds of things when you're kids; first how to build the boat, then how to maintain the motor, and finally the skills in terms of running the boat up and down the river. So we grew up in that part of the business. You know, one thing that really fascinated me was listening to the stories that my father would tell. As you know, he's a great storyteller.

Jim: Oh, yes!

Johne: He's just got such a tremendous memory for details and he has such a wonderful way of presenting stories.

Jim: It's poetry when he speaks, did you ever notice that about him? I remember one time he told me a story about how he was going up the Yukon, and he says, "Those purple fingers of light in the early morning made their way through the trees past the mountaintops." Who talks like that? Jim Binkley talks like that. It was just natural to him—it was beautiful. It was an interview on radio that was subsequently transcribed and presented in Volume I of Alaska Gold Trails. I have never forgotten that passage.

Johne: He's an extraordinary person. He really is. I just loved all of the stories he told, about the early days of freighting and his experiences working with Captain George Black, who was my father's real mentor. In the back of my mind, I always had this desire to live some of those days—the freighting days that he had. Because our business is very limited in terms of scope, and, of course, we are always taking passengers and never freight. We didn't have all of the challenges associated with hauling big loads over long distances and seeing vast amounts of territory of Alaska. So as we grew up in the passenger business I had a desire to enter the freighting business and have some of those experiences. You know, I was going to mention another thing, not to get off the subject too far, one place we learned a lot of our mechanical skills too, was very competitive by nature. My two brothers and I raced motorcycles and snowmachines as we were growing up, and that is where we learned a great deal about mechanics.

Jim: Competitive with one another or competitive all around?

Johne: All around. We competed with each other too. We raced motorcycles around town and around the state. The same with snowmachines.

Jim: Dirt bikes?

Johne: Dirt bikes, exactly, and snowmachines in the wintertime. So a big part of that, particularly in the early days, was mechanical skills, because snowmachines were not to the level of sophistication they are today. To have a competitive advantage, you had to modify those things and continually work on them. So we learned a lot of mechanical skills there as well. At any rate, I had this desire in the back of my mind to try and experience some of those same things that my father had always talked about. So after high school, I didn't go on to college. Instead I spent three years out in the states actually racing motorcycles and snowmachines professionally. I made a living at it.

Jim: What an exciting life that must have been.

Johne: Yes. It wasn't much of a living, but at least I supported myself. The first year, my brother Jim and I bought a camper and built an enclosed trailer, and we took our snowmachines and motorcycles and we drove down to the states, where we raced throughout Wisconsin, Michigan, Minnesota, all the way back through New York, as far west as West Yellowstone, Montana, and just had a tremendous time. The next year, I was hired by one of the factories and went back there and raced professionally for two more years.

Jim: They paid you?

Johne: Yeah, it was actually a paid position; I earned a living at it. It was a great experience.

Jim: Wonderful! Obviously you saw that it wasn't a lifelong activity.

Johne: No, no. I came back to Alaska, and then I drove my motorcycle from Prudhoe Bay to the tip of South America one winter. I left Prudhoe Bay December 2nd of 1975 and got down to Ushuaia in Tierra Del Fuego on April 21st of 1976. During that time, of course, there were 18,264 miles, I think, on my motorcycle odometer. You have hours and hours sitting alone on the motorcycle thinking. One of the things I thought about was, what I really wanted to do and that was to experience those freighting days my father always talked about. So when I came back from that motorcycle trip, I started to pursue what opportunities might be available in the freighting business. So in 1977, I started a little freight business. There was an opportunity that arose out of St. Marys on the lower Yukon River.

Jim: I remember hearing about that.

Johne: Yeah, Green Construction.

Jim: That's right.

Johne: The state wanted to improve some of the runways down in the Yukon-Kuskokwim Delta. They were just basically mud runways—no aggregate—no rock down there in the delta area of the Yukon-Kuskokwim. Any rock material for improving those runways had to be barged in. I saw an opportunity there and was able to lease an old tug. It was actually an old landing craft that had been used as a fish tender. I leased a couple of old junk barges and put the equipment together, and got a loan from the bank I got the sub-contract from Green Construction, and brought all the components of the business together.

Jim: You didn't have to go to Mom and Dad for help?

Johne: No I didn't, as a matter of fact. I went to the bank on my own for the loan—I think it was $25,000 to get enough working capital to put this all together—and got it going.

Jim: Good job, Johne!

Johne: It was interesting too. You know, my father, of course, wanted to help me. When we went to look at this little boat down in the village of Emmonuk on the lower Yukon River, we flew down there together, and here was this old landing craft, this fish tender, and they had just simply run it up on the mud in the fall and walked away from it. It was frozen down in the mud. The river had backed up, overflowed, and iced the whole thing in so that the whole thing, over the decks, was encased in ice. They hadn't drained down the engines. So one block was cracked. Both heads were cracked. The exhaust manifolds and the intake manifolds were all cracked. All the cooling systems were shot on the engines. The hull was rotten. The props were completely shot. The shafts...the gear boxes were the old-style gear boxes; they needed to be rebuilt. You know, it was interesting how we came upon this scene. It was wintertime down there, and we looked at this thing. What I saw when I looked at that was a beautiful boat that I could have. I could visualize myself on that thing, running this tugboat down the Yukon River, reliving some of those things my father always talked about. Now, my father looked at that and saw all of the work that was involved in it, because, of course he had so many years of experience. He knew what lay ahead in terms of the obstacles that would have to be overcome to actually make this happen. I didn't. I didn't have that experience, and all I saw was the end product of me on the Yukon River, captaining that tugboat, hauling a big load of gravel down the river. So our visions of it were completely different. He thought that maybe that wasn't the right thing to do, and he kind of cautioned me against that because of all that would be involved in making this tug work. But I had this tremendous vision of what it could be and was really ignorant of all the work it would take to get it operational. He didn't discourage me from it, but you know, our different perspectives were just so interesting. Despite his counsel, I decided to go forward with the project, which was okay with him. He was fine with that. He just didn't want me to get into something that I couldn't handle.

Jim: Johne, it seems that there are some things that we get 75 percent of the way into and we realize we can't handle, and we have to back out of it at a tremendous loss—not so much money, but you have lost valuable time and have gone nowhere in terms of your objective. Somebody once said to me, "Jim, every time you take on a project, first you have to fix your tools." I have to do that or I can't even start. I perceive that before you could get started, you were fixing your tools. Is that correct, Johne?

Johne: That is exactly right. I decided to go forward with it, because again I just didn't know what lay ahead of me. So I moved down to Emangak. I rented a little place from the N.C. (Northern Commercial) Company.

Jim: Were you married at that time?

Johne: I was not, although I was dating my wife. I moved right down there, had a honey bucket, pretty crude conditions. I hired a couple of kids to help me, from the village in Emmonuk. We chipped out all of the ice. It was an ordeal. Just looking back on it, I can't believe the amount of work it took to actually make that happen.

Jim: How long did it take you to get it running?

Johne: Well, I moved down there probably in April and began work. I didn't get the whole operation up and running until June. Might have even been late June by the time I finally got it going, so it was April, May, June, probably three months—a good solid three months—which included going through the breakup of the Yukon River down there with this thing frozen to the bottom; it flooded several times. I had to try and fly in parts. Then eventually I had to bring in one block. I had to have it barged down in June when the first barge came downriver. It was a long process. I had to haul the thing out. I found an old Cat (Caterpillar) in the village that wasn't running. I had to get that running and find some old block and tackle and skid some old log timbers up to work on the hull, the shafts, the stuffing boxes, bearings and props. The work was just endless. You know, I still kept in the back of my mind that vision of captaining that thing with a load coming down the Yukon River, and that's what kept me going. I was pretty tenacious about it. I wasn't going to give up or be discouraged.

Jim: Perhaps there was something else in the back of your mind as well; you couldn't, in the face of your father's suggestions, very well give this up.

Johne: That's right. I was going to succeed.

Jim: The old Binkley drive.

Johne: So at any rate, I started in the freight business. That summer Judy and I got married. That was in July of 1977. Then Judy cooked on the boat and I captained the boat. We had a local crew that we had hired from the villages there. It was exactly what I had dreamed about when I was on my motorcycle. That's how I pictured it. I pictured having a family and raising kids, living on the river, and having a wonderful life on the river running freight boats. So I started to really live that dream, and of course, it was much rougher and tougher conditions than was in my dreams.

Jim: Of course.

Johne: You know, we were getting stuck and you have breakdowns. When it was time to go berry picking the crew would take off.

Jim: In Australia, they call it " Go walkabout."

Johne: Yeah, walkabout. So it was a struggle. It wasn't easy by any means, but we worked our way through. We had a good season. We made a profit.

Jim: Wonderful! You mean after all of the rebuilding, you still made a profit?

Johne: Yes but it was mainly just my own labor. I'd hire a few people locally. My dad had a lot of the parts. They were 671 Detroit-Diesel engines, 8708 gear boxes. My dad collected parts from those things for years and years so he had all the parts that he basically gave me. So I got by cheap. I knew how to rebuild the Detroit engines and the gearboxes myself. The props, of course, I sent out and had rebuilt. I was able to do it on a shoestring just through a lot of hard work and effort and scrounging parts wherever I could.

Jim: Did you have minimal breakdowns, Johne?

Johne: No, as a matter of fact we had a lot of breakdowns and a lot of getting stuck. It was tough going. We got paid by the ton of gravel, so we tried to maximize the load all the time. The Yukon (River) down on the lower Yukon is wide and broad and there is the tidal effect and a lot of wind. It's difficult water to read, because the tide can affect the currents and the wind can distort a lot of the river patterns. So it's tough navigating down there. You can get pretty substantial weather too in the lower Yukon when the wind blows, coming right in off of the coast; it can result in some pretty heavy waves. Plus, we got a late start. It was late June or early July by the time we started. We had two airstrips to do that year, Emangak and Alakanuk. Green Construction helped a lot, once we got the barges there. They helped with steel that they had. Their welders used it to construct ramps for the barges so dump trucks could back up and dump their loads directly on the barge. They helped a lot in making the whole thing work.

Jim: Well, it sounds like everyone was working together to make the project a success.

Johne: Exactly.

Jim: Out in a country like that, you just can't be independent. Actually, in Alaska, in the early days, nobody was independent were they. They either worked with everybody else or they got themselves into trouble. Is that an accurate summary of early day experiences, Johne?

Johne: Right, exactly.

Jim: How many years did you run this operation, Johne?

Johne: Well, we ran the next year, in 1978, as well. Judy came back and cooked again on the boat, and I captained the boat. I'll never forget how she tells the story. The boat that year ended up on the coast. We ended up wintering it in Unalakleet, actually. Then, that spring, we went back to get the boat. I had a little T-Craft. We'd fly all the way out to the West Coast in that little T-Craft. It would take all day long. It would only go about 65 or 70 miles an hour. I had to get some parts. We brought the boat over to St. Michael and we had to do some work on it to haul some freight back to Unalakleet, but we needed some parts. I can't remember what they were. I got a local crew to run the boat from St. Michael over to Unalakleet. Then I flew from St. Michael all the way back to Fairbanks to get the parts, then flew back. Here Judy was pregnant on that boat. You know, you're kind of exposed out there going in this little landing craft with a couple of barges from St. Michael across Norton Sound. Here she was with a strange crew running this boat across open water, and I was flying away for Fairbanks, and she talks about how she was crying being left alone on this boat with a strange crew.

Jim: Pregnant and left on a barge with a strange crew. What a husband!

Johne: So anyhow, that year was tougher. We had to haul gravel all the way to Kotlik from St. Marys again. So we worked basically 1977 and 1978. Then in the summer of '78 we were successful with this program, so the state said, "We want to continue upgrading more of these runways in the Yukon-Kuskokwim Delta." So they decided to bid out eight more airports, basically closer toward the Kuskokwim on the coastal area between the deltas, but out of the Kuskokwim area. I bid on the subcontract to haul gravel from Bethel up to those coastal villages on the Kuskokwim River. Kind of a long story, but eventually I got the work.

Jim: You were awarded all of them?

Johne: Got all eight. One general contractor got all eight to construct the runways. Then we were able to get a subcontract with them to do the barging. That was a huge jump; we went from having one tugboat and two barges that Judy and I basically ran, to eventually having five tugboats and crews and multiple barges.

Jim: Oh-oh.

Johne: It was much more complicated too. We had to barge the gravel from near Aniak on the Kuskokwim River, down to Bethel, then off-load the barges. There Kink Construction, which was owned by Jim Jansen—the Jansen family and Lynden Transport had the general contract—they would crush the material to meet the specs that they needed. Then we would reload it on coastward barges that we would take out to the coastal areas to deliver to the communities where they would reconstruct those runways. So it was a big operation. At that point, Judy and I had to get off the boats to manage all this.

Jim: That's why I made the little comment, "Oh-oh," because I could see that the paperwork was going to become overwhelming. The management requirements would overshadow the enjoyment you were looking for originally.

Johne: Exactly. That's exactly right! I lost sight of that goal that I had for Judy and me and our family to be on the boat. It really got away from me. Then I was really managing, and we were both off of the boat. We had a baby that fall in 1978, our oldest son Ryan. So then in '79 we moved to Bethel from St. Marys and started the operation there. Judy ran the office, and she had an infant to care for and I was constantly on the go. I was in my plane flying just to keep up with the needs of those boats, managing everything and making certain the operation ran smoothly. It's amazing how different it was from when Judy and I were running the single boat ourselves, to managing an operation with five separate captains and first mates and deckhands and crew and mechanics. The efficiency just drops dramatically, because when you are doing everything yourself, you can do it so much more efficiently.

Jim: You get into a rhythm with yourself. You can't hold that rhythm together when you have too many people making even tiny operational decisions.

Johne: We grew up where we did everything ourselves, and we took such good care of everything. We had the same head line on the boat for 15 years, because we took care of that line, made sure it wasn't chafing on anything. We were careful with it. The tools were all in the right place. We took real good care of everything. When you start hiring crews, they don't have that same care for the equipment, and you're going through snapping cables and lines, and outboard motor boats that get smashed between the tug and the barges and sink, and pumps that get knocked overboard. It's endless, tools that get lost. It just costs so much more. You just can't always hire people that have the same drive and desire you do, and the care that you have for your own business. It was a whole new experience for us. We completely got away from what we originally wanted to start doing. It was like a snowball going down the hill. We were kind of running after it trying to keep up.

Jim: How long did you run the operation?

Johne: Well, we had the small operation, and it began to evolve. First, we were just hauling gravel during the original operation which in itself was a monstrous undertaking. But later, I bought Black Navigation's operation out in Bethel to get the equipment to start the larger operation. They had been hauling freight and fuel out of Bethel for some time, competing with another local company in Bethel called United Transportation. They basically weren't able to make it out there against the competition, so they pulled all of their equipment together and they were leaving Bethel. They were going to bring all of that equipment home—forklifts, cranes, conveyors, hoppers, barges, tugs, vehicles, everything. They had it all loaded up on barges and they were bringing it out the mouth of the Kuskokwim. They intended to bring it around the coast into the mouth of the Yukon and up all the way to Nenana, but when they went out, they got caught in a storm. Some of the equipment sank and much of the equipment that didn't sink got beat up. Barges got holes punched in them. It was a scattered mess. They limped the whole fleet back into Bethel. It was fall time, and the late start was one of the reasons they hit bad weather out in the Bering Sea. So they tied everything up and walked away from it. Well, that winter I negotiated with them to buy all of that equipment and property that they had in Bethel, because I needed it to handle the movement of gravel for the new contracts. So I bought all of this equipment from them. I got a great deal, because they had gotten a big insurance settlement. A lot of it was just junk, really run down over the years, and beat up, but even so, I then had additional and useful freight-handling equipment, including cranes and forklifts, along with good property right on the riverbank, and of equal importance, an I.C.C. license. At that time, we still had the Interstate Commerce Commission, and we had to have the license to haul freight with a tariff. We had fuel barges and-fuel handling equipment, but I focused primarily on gravel, because that's what our contract was. So as we completed our gravel contract. I started fixing up the other equipment and then started to haul freight and bulk petroleum fuel to the villages up and down the Kuskokwim River. So we evolved from just gravel into the freight and fuel side of the business as well. We continued to grow and expand and build the business. As you may know, Jim, you are paid by the ton for freight, by the gallon for fuel and of course by the ton for the gravel. So you're always loading your vessels as deep as you can possibly load them; it is important to carry as big a payload as you can possibly handle without getting stuck. So that's a fine line to always run. You miss it a lot of times and you get stuck. Then you're working to try and get the equipment off the river bars. It's a time when you've got more potential for the crew to get hurt and injured, because you're working long hours, and there's a lot of stress and a lot of big, heavy equipment that's swinging around. So there's a lot of things going on and a lot of opportunity to get injured out there when you're doing those sorts of things. We were running 24 hours a day, seven days a week. There were crew and provisioning problems, breakdowns out in the middle of nowhere, weather on the Bering Sea coast, and tides. It's a tough tough business.

Jim: You spoke about people getting hurt. Did you have or do you know of any serious accidents?

Johne: I know one fellow broke his ankle. He got in the bite of a line when we were stuck and broke his ankle really bad. In fact, our brother-in-law, Judy's brother, worked for us and broke his leg pretty bad. I think those were the only two major accidents we had, but it always worried me.

Jim: Well in ten years it wasn't a bad record really.

Johne: It's not a bad record at all. It can be dangerous. I know our competitor out there had three people killed, actually—one of the owners, as a matter of fact. Terrible accident. It was a fuel barge that they were getting ready for the spring Coast Guard inspection. There are valves that are on the top of each tank that allow the fumes and pressure to vent off. Usually there are expansion tanks and vents over each of the tanks, but in this one the vents were all piped to a common area. It was an ocean-going barge and the vent had to be pulled off every spring for the Coast Guard inspection to make certain that it was functioning properly. Usually these can be wrenched off using a big pipe wrench. But this one, because it had been out in the salt water, was stuck, and it wouldn't break loose, and just not thinking, the fellow took a torch to heat that up and break it loose.

Jim: Oh my! I am starting to get a picture of what was about to happen.

Johne: It happened to be the vent for a tank that had gasoline in it left from the previous fall—just a couple of inches of gas in the bottom. It was a warm spring day and as a result the tank was completely full of gas fumes, and as soon as he touched that torch to the valve where the fumes were venting, it flashed back and exploded that compartment—blew the entire section out and killed three of the guys. I've never seen such power—3/8-inch steel plating, heavy scantlings and ribs required for ocean-going barges—it just ripped that steel completely out, tearing the section right down the middle of the bulkhead, the sides and across the deck and then down the sides to the keel. Blew that whole section. It probably weighed 10—15 tons. All that steel just blew completely out. It flew over 50 feet, hit another tug that was a ways up on the shore, and bounced down again—just tremendous power, and of course killed those three men that were working on the barge. That accident has always stuck in the back of my mind.

Jim: It is not hard to understand how something like that might stick in your memory for the rest of your life. Let's change direction here, Johne. When and where did you get involved in politics?

Johne: Bethel is where Judy and I lived and raised our children, and that is where I got involved in politics. It started with an interest and concern with what was going on in our community. I was elected to the Bethel City Council. It was while I was on the city council that they talked me into running for the state House of Representatives. After serving two years as a state representative, I ran for the (state of Alaska) senate and represented quite a large area out there. I had envisioned I could do as my father had when we were kids. He was in the legislature. He came home in the spring, and we ran our business, and in the winter he went down to Juneau and they were in session for about 90 days. It worked out fine. He was gone for a period of time, but he came back, got the boats fired up in the spring, and he could run the business that way. But as I got into it, there was no way I could run the operation and still do a good job on the legislative side in representing that area. So in 1986, there was an opportunity to sell the business to Crowley Maritime. They are a huge, big company, and they were coming into Bethel. Rather than try and compete, we merged into one operation. Then I eventually sold my interest to them and we were out of the barge business completely. That was 1986, I think, when I finally sold it. So basically, we ran from the season of 1977 to 1986. We operated ten seasons living out our dream.

Jim: Were you satisfied that you had actually lived out that dream, Johne?

Johne: Yes. Oh, I loved it! It was just tremendous. You know, just a lot of those same memories of stories my father would tell me about getting stuck on river sandbars and how they would get off. Those were the same things that I lived during those ten years. Watching those beautiful sunrises and sunsets while I was up there alone in the wheelhouse. It is so peaceful and beautiful at three o'clock in the morning, running up there on the river when the sun is just coming up. It was great, and working with the native people in the villages up and down the river was just wonderful.

Jim: Those were the same words that your father used ten years ago when we were having our interview on the radio.

Johne: Interesting.

Jim: It's basically the enjoyment of the people, the scenery and the land.

Johne: It really is.

Jim: You have many of your father's fine qualities, Johne?

Johne: Well, that's a high compliment.

Jim: Was it in 1987 that you came back to Fairbanks?

Johne: No, I was in the state senate so I didn't come back until I had finished my senate term.

Jim: When was that over, Johne?

Johne: That was over in 1991. It was a tough choice because I loved the legislature. I really enjoyed politics, but the situation was that I would have had to run for another four-year term, which would have been through 1995. Our oldest son, at that point, was in the sixth grade. That would've meant that he would have been in high school by the time my term was up again. We had moved the kids between school in Bethel and school in Juneau, because I would take the whole family with me when the legislature was in session. I didn't want to leave them behind in Bethel. As the kids got older, it got tougher and tougher to make that change every year. Particularly in high school, I think that it would have been tough for them to spend half a year in Bethel, and half a year in Juneau. So we made the decision that our first priority was really our children and our family. We needed to stabilize and get out of politics while the kids were going through high school. So Judy and I made a decision not to run again in 1990, and then the question was where do we want to be for those years while our kids are growing up? Judy was born and raised here in Fairbanks. So her family was here, and, of course, my family was here. We had sold the business by that time. So we decided well, we'll move back to Fairbanks, work back into the family business, and that would give us a place to be stable while the kids went through high school and grew up, and they would have an opportunity to be around their aunts, uncles, cousins and grandparents.

Jim: How did the children feel about this decision? Were they excited about coming back to Fairbanks?

Johne: They were fine. They liked it. We had come back sometimes in the summer to give them a chance to work in the business, and they loved it. Summers in Fairbanks are beautiful. I think they would've been happy wherever we went, but they enjoyed coming back to Fairbanks, and again being with their cousins and grandparents and that sort of thing. That's how we ended up moving back to Fairbanks in 1990 and then getting back into the passenger business from the freight business. It was interesting too, to go from the passenger business when I was growing up, to the freight business, and then back to the passenger business. In many regards, this is easier, because your freight walks on and walks off. They have a ticket. It was nice to get into the passenger business. It was particularly nice to work with family.

Jim: What year did you construct and transport Discovery III into Fairbanks?

Johne: That was 1987. I was still living in Bethel.

Jim: But you were part of that operation?

Johne: Oh yeah. My oldest brother, Skip, and several of our friends ran that boat from St. Marys on up to Fairbanks. I had to actually get off at one point, because the governor had called us into special session. So I had to jump off of the boat in Galena, and then fly down to Juneau for that special session. Transporting Discovery III to Fairbanks was a great trip.

Jim: Tell us about what you have been doing since 1990. What direction do you see your life taking?

Johne: Well, for my wife and me, our number one focus has been raising our family. That's our number one job, so we don't forget that.

Jim: That's the exact words your father said to me, and your mother said something similar.

Johne: Really?

Jim: Yes, exactly. He said, "It's all family."

Johne: Yes, it is. Well they've instilled that in us, and through their example we learned that there is no greater calling than being a parent and raising our children. That's been our focus. Other than that, we've been working in the business. I worked quite a number of years—I think the first three years—as the commentator on the riverboat *Discovery*, which was a great experience and very enjoyable. More recently we've been involved with the Eldorado Gold Mine. In 1992, I believe it was, we took over full ownership of it. We then invested a substantial amount of money to expand it and build it up.

Jim: What is your direct role in the gold mine, Johne?

Johne: I took over management of that operation too. First in building it up. There was a tremendous amount of expansion involved in upgrading and rebuilding the operation, so I changed the format a little and expanded it. Both Judy and I ran that operation for a number of years, and then I began training a general manager. Jason Kowalchuk now runs the operation, and Judy backed out of it as well. Then she took over all of the retail operations for riverboat gift shops when we moved out of El Dorado into the riverboat side of things. In addition too that, we are teaching our kids the art of riverboat captaining, piloting and general work on the river. They first worked at the gold mine for a time, then relocated to the riverboat side of the business. They served as deckhands then moved up through all the different aspects of riverboating. Outside of that, I've been involved in some public service areas on various boards and commissions. I serve on the board of directors for the Alaska Railroad Corporation; I think that this is my sixth or seventh year. Currently I serve as chairman of the board for the Railroad Corporation, which I really enjoy. It has been a fascinating learning experience.

Jim: Learning is an enjoyable experience in itself, isn't it?

Johne: Very enjoyable, but you know what? You wouldn't think it, but out at El Dorado, we have a small, narrow-gauge train. Everything that we do is on a much smaller scale, but it's just exactly the same as the Alaska Railroad in terms of ballast and ties and rail and curvature, track structure and switches, locomotive power, all the safety aspects. It's amazing, our little train operation is a miniature of the Alaska Railroad.

Jim: Where is El Dorado?

Johne: It's about a mile north of Fox on the Elliott Highway.

Jim: About 11 miles from Fairbanks?

Johne: Yes. Correct. North of Fairbanks.

Jim: What is the attraction at the El Dorado Gold Mine, aside from the railroad, which you have already mentioned?

Johne: What we really try to do is give visitors information and knowledge about the history of mining in Interior Alaska and about modern-day mining, and talk about how that related to the economy and the development of Alaska in its infancy as gold was discovered in this area, and how it continues today to be a driving force in our economy. We try to present it in a way that shows the best of placer mining and how it is compatible with life here in Alaska, and how it is environmentally sound, and how we, as a society rely on the development of our minerals, and how it is important that we develop minerals in Alaska. We try to send that message in an entertaining and a pleasing way so that people are not only gaining knowledge but they are having fun while they are learning. An important element is the fact that it is interactive—they get to participate by actually gold panning. So the format of the trip is to use the train, which is a replica of the early Tanana Valley Railroad, which ran from the steamboats on the river through the Goldstream Valley and up over into the Chatanika Valley and into Chatanika. We use that as the means of conveying to people early rail transportation in the area. They board the narrow-gauge train, and as we take them out to our modern mining operation, we explain the history and the methods of early-day drift mining in Interior Alaska. When we get out to the camp, that's where Yukon Yonda and Dexter Clark meet the visitors and explain the methods of modern-day placer mining. Of course, as you know, they're wonderful individuals and have a great way of presenting mining and their stories. So people are excited about it and they're interested. It's fun and it's very informative at the same time. The culmination is really when the visitors get a chance to take some of that concentrate that we run through the sluicebox and actually do the panning themselves. It's so neat to see how excited the visitors from around the world get when they see the first gold in the bottom of their pan. It's timeless; that same excitement is there today as it was 100 years ago when the first prospectors discovered gold in the Tanana Valley.

Jim: Yes, I've seen it happen. Speaking of the early miners and their methods, don't you have a drift mine set up so that people can see how drift mining operated in the early days?

Johne: Exactly. We can't actually take people underground, because there would be too many complications to it. So we've constructed something that really replicates that. They feel like they are going underground. They get a sense of what it is like underneath there, and we can show a large number of people at the same time what it's like underground. For people to understand it, they need to see it first hand. You can try and explain it to them, but when they actually see it and the machinery in operation—such as the steam engine that's bringing a muck bucket up out of a shaft and up the highline, tripping and dumping the muck, coming back down and going down the shaft—they start to understand how it all actually works. Then when they see the operation, where the excavator is dumping the gravel from the drift into the hopper and the water is running down the sluicebox, and they can see it work, it really starts to make sense. Finally, when we pull the test riffle to check for gold, they understand placer mining. It's interesting too because so many people have a misconception of gold mining. Maybe it's been from news commentators or things that they have heard or read over the years, but when they actually see this operation themselves, I think they form a different opinion about gold mining, especially placer mining in Alaska. I think that they see that it's not anything that pillages the countryside and makes a big mess. They realize that miners are just as concerned about the environment as other people and want to preserve it. By the time they have completed the tour their perception of mining in Alaska has been changed; they realize we love Alaska and want to maintain its beauty and we can extract minerals and do it in a way that is compatible with the environment. They walk away with a completely different understanding, a first-hand personal experience that is much more meaningful than reading something somebody else wrote and how they may try to portray mining.

Jim: Let's get back to how all that early mining equipment was transported into the country. Riverboating has played a big role in the Binkley family life. How many riverboats do you have?

Johne: We have three sternwheelers: *Discovery, Discovery II* and *Discovery III.*

Jim: Do they all operate, or do you keep one in reserve?

Johne: They are all operating, fully functional operating passenger sternwheelers. We only run *Discovery II* and *Discovery III* in our normal tour operations. *Discovery* is much smaller, and we use that primarily for training for the grandkids, also for family picnics, or for outings or special events we may have. It runs just like a champion. My dad has restored it over the years. It's kind of fun to have. My mom and dad keep it parked in front of their house on the Chena River and enjoy looking at it every day.

Jim: And reminisce?

Johne: Yeah, they do. It's fun for Dad too, because he built the whole thing. He took pieces and parts from other boats.

Jim: Was that your first boat?

Johne: No, the *Godspeed* was our first boat.

Jim: That was the little, tiny one.

Johne: Yes, it was a little missionary boat.

Jim: Which one was George Black's boat?

Johne: *Discovery II* was originally built by George Black in 1953. It was the last of the stern-wheel-powered freight boats. It was a paddle wheeler, designed by George, that would push barges up and down the Tanana and Yukon Rivers. It didn't really work out very well. It was at the tail end, and the prop-driven boats were coming into fashion at that time— diesel-powered, propeller-driven boats. They were much more efficient for pushing big loads and barges. It was easier to get higher horsepowers with the propeller-driven boats. Yutana Barge Lines used Black's boat for awhile to ferry vehicles back and forth across the river before the George Parks Highway bridge was built in Nenana. When the bridge was completed, they just put the boat up in storage, on the bank, and just left it. Then my father bought it, I think in about 1967 or '68. It was just rusting away there on the riverbank. We brought it up to Fairbanks, completely rebuilt it, repowered it, rebuilt the wheel, changed all of the machinery, jacked up the decks to give more headroom between the decks, completely redid the mechanical, the electrical and all aspects of it. We finally put it into service in 1971 as *Discovery II*—replacing *Discovery*. It wasn't long before we started to outgrow *Discovery II*, so we began running both *Discovery* and *Discovery II* in tandem trips with staggered departures, in order to keep up with demand. It was clear that we had to build another vessel. So we contracted to have that vessel built by Nichols Brothers, a family operation on Whidbey Island in Puget Sound near Seattle. We designed *Discovery III*, and my oldest brother, Skip, stayed right in the shipyard as it was being built. It was completed in the spring of 1987. Then we brought it up, ran it up the Yukon River and put it into operation in 1987. We had enough capacity on *Discovery III* to lay up both *Discovery II* and *Discovery*.

Jim: How many passengers could each of the vessels handle?

Johne: *Discovery* is licensed for 150 passengers

Jim: And *Discovery II*?

Johne: Four hundred passengers, and *Discovery III* can handle 900 passengers.

Jim: And today you're running both *Discovery II* and *Discovery III*?

Johne: That's right. The business has grown. Although we are licensed for 900 passengers on *Discovery III*, we try to hold the loads to 700 passengers maximum. We have just over 1,000 seats on the boat, but with 700 passengers, there's almost 50 percent empty seats. So people feel like they have a little bit more room. They can move around or try a different seat if they want to. So, although we could push it higher, we think that the quality starts to deteriorate if we do. The loads have grown so that we needed to bring on the second vessel. Rather than build another boat, *Discovery IV*, we took *Discovery II*, which had really been setting for many years not doing anything, and refurbished it completely, bringing it up to the same high quality mechanical standards as *Discovery III*. We put bow thrusters on it, stern thrusters to get better maneuverability, re-did all of the mechanical systems, the electrical and the water systems. The standards have been changed by the Coast Guard—including advanced fire suppression systems because it had to be licensed as though it was a new vessel. We brought that on last season, in the summer of 2000, with a limited amount of use—primarily some charters to get all of the bugs worked out of it, to make sure it was working well—and in this year, 2001, we went to staggered departures just like we had with *Discovery II* and *Discovery*. Now we are doing that with *Discovery III* and *Discovery II*. That really gives us a lot more capacity. Even though we are licensed for 400, we like to keep that to 300 so that gives us a comfortable capacity of 1,000 people twice a day.

Jim: How long of a season do you have, and are you filling 1000 a day?

Johne: Well there are occasions that we do. The season still peaks in mid-July to mid-August. There is still definitely a shoulder to the season, although it improves. It used to be a dramatic spike before, with the tremendous ramp up to the peak and a tremendous drop-off from the peak. Actually, the shoulders have broadened out so you don't have quite as steep a peak in the middle of the season. We are not full every day by any means.

Jim: When is your busiest season? In July around Golden Days?

Johne: Yes, I'd say mid-July to mid-August is the peak time. Although now it's heavy traffic even in mid-June through August. But we still peak in that one-month period between mid-July and mid-August. We operate about 120 days, mid-May to mid-September, right in that area. What really started to drive a lot of the numbers now are the cruise ship visitors. We get a large number of visitors that come up on cruise ships to Seward and then come up over the railbelt, usually motorcoach to Anchorage and rail up to Fairbanks, and then fly home or return home in reverse—they fly into Fairbanks, take the rail down to Anchorage, motorcoach to Seward, get on the cruise ship down in Seward, go down through Southeast (Alaska) and end up in Vancouver. So that has really brought a larger volume of passengers through Fairbanks. The cruise ships, of course, have a certain number of beds and capacity when they leave Vancouver, and they like to be full, because their fixed costs are virtually the same whether they are full or empty. It's advantageous for them, if they are not going to be full, to drop their pricing in order to fill those cruise ship berths. So that has really helped in bringing a steadier flow of visitors to Fairbanks and the whole system. They can move some of the demand for those sailings to Alaska by pricing. So they'll have a more expensive pricing in the peak of the season, then they'll cut the price for the shoulders, and so that is an incentive for people to get a better value by going early or going late. It really has helped to smooth out the peaks and valleys somewhat.

Jim: Just quickly, Johne, what do you have planned for the future?

Johne: Well, our oldest son has graduated from college. We have two in college. Our daughter will graduate this spring. Then we have one son left in high school. So, of course, once the kids are through school—and we are getting pretty close to that—I might get involved with politics again. As I mentioned, I really enjoyed it. I felt good about what I was able to accomplish.

Jim: How's Alaska treated you?

Johne: Oh, the land of opportunity.

Jim: I really have enjoyed our interview, Johne. It has been a lot of fun reminiscing this way. We will hear from you again during the Felix Pedro roundtable discussion.

Johne: Well I've enjoyed it too Jim and look forward to the Felix Pedro discussion.

Terrence Cole
with
Jim Madonna
October 23, 2001

Jim: Today our traveling microphone has followed the trail to the University of Alaska Fairbanks where we are meeting with Terrence Cole. Welcome to Alaska Gold Trails, Terrence.

Terrence: Thanks, Jim. I am looking forward to the interview.

Jim: Later we are going to discuss the founding of Fairbanks and the life of Felix Pedro, but first, Terrence, let's get a little background on you—where you came from, when you were born, and how you happened to become a history professor at the University of Alaska Fairbanks.

Terrence: I was born in Pennsylvania in 1953 and have a twin brother. We are identical twins. We grew up in a large family. I have six brothers and sisters. I came to Alaska when I was 16 years old with my oldest brother, Pat. He was three years older than Dermot and I. The reason we came to Alaska is in some ways interesting. He had been mugged in Philadelphia. He was going to college down there and had been really badly beaten. After he got out of the hospital, the way he always tells this wellworn story is that he went to the library to find another place to go to college as far away from Philadelphia as possible. He started with the college catalogs; they were all alphabetically listed by state. He didn't want to go to Alabama...so that's how he and I ended up in Alaska a year later in 1970. We drove up here. I stayed for a month or so with him, and I really loved the place. Subsequent to that time my family moved from Pennsylvania to Taiwan, where my father was an engineer for Ford Motor Company. I spent a year with them overseas. I graduated from high school in Taiwan. Then I went to college for one year in Hong Kong before I came back up here with one of my two younger sisters. We started at the University together in 1972. Over the years, five of my brothers and sister attended the University of Alaska. Eventually four of us ended up graduating, and three of us still live in Fairbanks, 30 years later. My oldest brother, Pat, who was the one I drove up with in 1970, is a local attorney, and Dermot, my twin brother, works for the Fairbanks Daily News-Miner.

Jim: How did you get interested in history, specifically the history of Fairbanks?

Terrence: I got interested in Alaska history from the very beginning because it just fascinated me, and I thought it was so tangible here, unlike anything that I'd ever known as a kid back east where it seems so old and distant. And now, looking back, I guess it was probably my own youthful ignorance. Commonly, when people grow up in an area where there's lots of history, many times they take it for granted because they think that's sort of the way things were. But I knew, being an immigrant here, it wasn't always this way. So it instantly intrigued me in a way that I'd never been interested in history on the Outside, and only subsequently going back to Pennsylvania, where my family still has a farm, have I seen that there is a lot of interesting history there. It is just a lot older. Our house that I grew up in was built in the 18th century. We always knew that, "Well so what?" Which is, in a way, like some of the local people perceive Fairbanks. Somebody who was born here or maybe even arrived when they were a little younger might not be as intrigued by it as somebody who comes upon it new or in a little bit later stage of life. Lots of times, when you're born in a place, you think you know what it is all about because it is your formative years, but I can honestly say, for me, that I became just fascinated by Alaskan history, and I love to hike and walk around, find old cabins and stuff like that. That's how I first got interested in the history of Fairbanks.

Jim: When you first enrolled at the university was it as a history major?

Terrence: No, actually I started out studying geography here at the university. I got into history when I started in the master's program. I first wanted to write a thesis on the Tanana Valley Railroad, the narrow-gauge railroad from Chena and Fairbanks up to Chatanika, because I was interested in railroads—all railroads. Dermot and I had hiked a lot of the old railroad trail, and there were still a lot of interesting remnants there. I remember taking a picture of this one spot, then when the Trans-Alaska oil Pipeline was under construction, in 1975, and they were constructing it down over the hill on the other side of Fox, and it crossed that spot on the Tanana Valley Railroad, I can't remember if there were any abutments that they actually had to bulldoze away to construct the pipeline or not. I thought, "This is amazing: Here is this brand new construction of the Trans-Alaska oil Pipeline—this giant engineering project intersecting this ancient railroad that used to be so vital, and yet people don't even remember it."

Jim: When you think about it, there were two vital projects constructed in precisely the same spot. It is an intriguing thought that both projects had the common purpose of transportation. The only thing separating them was time. Thinking about that time separation and the technology of each period as well as the prevailing social atmosphere must have been fascinating to you from a historical perspective.

Terrence: Yes, it was. The more I went into it, the more intriguing it was. But, as you know, research projects have a habit of changing.

Jim: I know it well. Many times an investigator is required to alter the course of the research as they uncover new information that sheds a different light on the subject. Tell us what happened; you're leading up to something.

Terrence: Even though I was still interested in the railroad, and Falcon Joslin, the builder of it, and the physical remains of the railroad, the project changed. As you pointed out, a lot of research projects do. It evolved into writing about E.T. Barnette. My original idea was to use the Tanana Valley Railroad as the vehicle for telling the story of the history of Fairbanks and the surrounding mining camps. Then I realized that a better vehicle might be E.T. Barnette himself, because there was not really much known about him, and so much of it was very contradictory. I still remember a picture that Frank Young believed was E.T. Barnette, and I thought, "Geez, I don't think that's who that is." There was very little written about Barnette at that time. Bill Cashen had written a very nice, sort of brief treatment of the history of Fairbanks, and had noted that everybody in Fairbanks always said that Barnette was convicted of embezzling money from his bank when it went broke, and then skipped town. I thought, "Well, this is an interesting thing. So, what happened to this guy?" Like I said, there was this debate over who was in this picture, and Frank said it was this one guy, other people said it was other people. This famous picture of the bankers of Fairbanks—they're all lined up behind a big shipment of gold dust heading outside from the First National Bank of Fairbanks, and Fairbanks Banking Company which was Barnette's banking company at the time. It's a really great picture, but anyway there's one very shifty-eyed character, and that's who a lot of people were identifying as E.T. Barnette. As I looked into this mystery about him—maybe not mystery, maybe lack of knowledge— I learned we didn't know how old he was when he was here, didn't know his exact name. He went by "E.T." Some people said it was Elbridge, some said his name was Ebenezzer. So we didn't know where he was born; we didn't know his name; we didn't know what he looked like; we didn't know where he died, and we didn't really know hardly anything about this guy at all. So my focus shifted from the railroad to Barnette.

Jim: How did you shift back to the point where Felix Pedro came into the picture?

Terrence: Looking back on it, I wish I'd done more, in a way, with both Pedro and Wickersham. These two people are really key to the development of Fairbanks. The emphasis of my thesis and then my book was a biography/history of Fairbanks using Barnette on the one hand and the city on the other—it was like two mirrors in that they reflected off each other, and using Fairbanks as the vehicle to tell Barnett's story and Barnett's life story to tell Fairbanks' early story. So I focused more on Barnette. I brought him to the fore more than either Felix Pedro or Judge Wickersham. I think Bill Cashen's interpretation was very astute I just don't think I realized it at the time. It was years ago, but he talked about there being three founders of Fairbanks: Barnette, Felix Pedro and Judge Wickersham. There's a lot to that I think, because the city of Fairbanks would not have existed unless all three intersected with each other. So I think, Jim, looking back, I wish I would've done more with Pedro, but my early history of Fairbanks is focused more on Barnette because he was the bigger mystery.

Jim: Indeed he was. We will cover these three people in more detail when we discuss the life of Felix Pedro a little later in this book. I think you will agree, Terrence, that it would be difficult, if not impossible, to discuss the life of one of these people without touching on the lives of the other two as you did. Correct me if I am wrong, but your thesis was titled *The Story of Captain E.T. Barnette: A Narrative History of Fairbanks, Alaska,* and the book that followed was *E.T. Barnette,* and finally it was recently republished as *Crooked Past.* Is that correct?

Terrence: Yes. The modified thesis was first published as *E.T. Barnette* by

Alaska Northwest Publishing Company in 1981, then as *Crooked Past* by University of Alaska Press in 1991.

Jim: *Crooked Past* can be found in local bookstores. I enjoyed it every time I read it. Thank you for taking time to share this information with us, Terrence, and we will be back with you when we get together to discuss the life of Felix Pedro.

Terrence: I am looking forward to it, Jim.

Shann Jones
with
Jim Madonna
July 19, 2002

Jim: We haven't traveled very far today. We are here in Fairbanks, Alaska, interviewing my guest, Shann Paul Jones. Shann, tell us a little about your background, beginning with when and where you were born.

Shann: Well Jim, I was born February 6th, 1966, in Johnstown, Pennsylvania. That's about 60 miles east of Pittsburgh, Pennsylvania, right in the middle of the historic Chestnut Ridge, Appalachian coal district.

Jim: Were you a country boy raised in the Appalachian Mountains?

Shann: It was about as country living in that valley as a person can get. Robinson, the town I grew up in, was about 800 people.

Jim: What did your father do?

Shann: My father started out as a schoolteacher, and later spent some time working in the underground coal mines in the area, and then went back to teaching high school. He was also the wrestling coach at United Area Joint Junior-Senior High School, for 19 years. He taught special education. He taught junior high government. He taught Pennsylvania history, and I believe for awhile he taught American history. Unfortunately, he passed away last October 1.

Jim: Sorry to hear that. That was October 1, 2001. Give us a little background on your mother. What did she do all those years?

Shann: My mother stayed at home and raised my brother and me until 1975. About that time she got involved with developing a local ambulance service. Previously there wasn't any in the area. They started out as a bunch of trained volunteers. In 1983 she became a medic and rose in certification to the level of Paramedic 1, and sat on the board of directors for Tri-Community Ambulance. I believe she's going on about 20 years as a paramedic.

Jim: You said she raised you and your brother for awhile. Who's younger, you or your brother?

Shann: My brother Derek is five-and-a-half years younger than I am. He was almost six when my mother went to work at the local store that was about 150 yards from our house. She worked there while we were in school. She worked the morning shift as a short-order cook in their deli.

Jim: How long did she hold that job?

Shann: About eight years.

Jim: Was that before she became a paramedic?

Shann: Well, she was doing the volunteering on the ambulance at the same time, and then when they started to get into paid positions, I think she left the store and started working more with the ambulance service in Bolivar, which is only about a mile from Robinson, just across the Conemaugh River.

Jim: Your brother must have been about 10 or 11 years old when your mother got fully involved with the ambulance?

Shann: That's right, Jim.

Jim: Tell us about your schooling. Did you go to the school in that town?

Shann: In Robinson, yes. It was kind of funny. The Garfield Elementary schoolhouse was two buildings down, and across the street, from my grandparents' house. Now the funniest thing I remember was when I was in kindergarten. I was the kid that everything always happened to—got sick in the lunchroom or fell. The school nurse had my folk's number in the front of her phone list, I think. I can remember one particular time I was in kindergarten; the teacher called us in from recess. The playground was situated behind the school. Right up against the back of the brick school was an asphalt basketball court. So I started to sprint into the schoolhouse, but the kindergarten classroom was in the basement near the front of the building. Now that old school house was heated with coal. Somehow the truck was up there and left some coal ash and cinder on the basketball court. So I slipped in it, fell and cracked my head open. Instead of calling my mother to come and take me home— I lived in a town where everybody really did know everybody, and many of the people were related in some way, Jim—they called my grandmother—I think Grandpap was working afternoon shift at the mine. They just walked me over to her house. I remember my dad coming in. He got off work from teaching school at that time at about three o'clock in the afternoon. So he would've been there by about four. I'm sitting there with an ice bag on my head—one of those old cloth types that had a screw-on metal lid that you actually put ice cubes into. He asked me, "What happened?" "I fell and cracked my head open," I said. That's all I could come up with. I didn't get any stitches or anything.

Jim: Tell me another one. Did you ever break any bones?

Shann: No, I never broke any bones when I was a kid. I remember one time when I was in high school. I was playing pick-up basketball on the same court. By this time the school district had consolidated all of the elementary schools, and the junior-senior high schools, which, by the way, was the same one my dad taught at. They were about ten miles away. Anyway, I was playing basketball, and I went to save a ball from going out of bounds. I rolled up my ankle, and I thought for sure I had broken it. It turned out to be a really bad sprain. So my friend Brian Litchenfels hauls me down the hill to my house (my family moved into my grandparents' house after my dad's father died in 1974). I was heavily involved with Future Farmers of America. We were doing a lot of studies with forestry and trees, and we had a county forestry competition coming up. My mother said something to the effect that I was going to have to miss the event. There wasn't any way I was skipping out of that competition. About three or four days later was the competition, which required that we go out and estimate tree height and usable board feet in a stand of lumber. There I am out there hobbling along on crutches, going through the woods doing all of this. I can't remember how we placed as a team. I know I didn't earn any individual honors that day, but I wasn't going to let a little thing like a severely sprained ankle stop me. I just strapped on a good heavy boot I borrowed from my brother.

Jim: Is your little brother bigger than you?

Shann: The last time I talked to my brother, he was 5 feet 7 inches tall and tipping the scale at 170 pounds

Jim: How tall are you?

Shann: Five feet, four inches and 130 pounds—a runt!

Jim: You're a short guy, aren't you? You're an Italian?

Shann: Semi—my maternal grandfather is Italian.

Jim: Did he come from Italy?

Shann: He came from Sicily, actually. He's 91 years old now. His name is Salvatore Bucceri. He is alive and doing quite well. He's an interesting person. He worked on the railroad in Pennsylvania near a town called Seward for 47 years, starting in 1929. I thought it was interesting he was able to start working around the time that the Great Depression started. Over the years, railroad workers get laid off from time to time. He had a second occupation; he was a barber. He started barbering in Floridia, Sicily, in 1917 when he was six years old. He finally hung up his scissors in 1982. So he was barbering for 65 years.

Jim: Did he have to go to barber school over here, or was it on-the-job training?

Shann: I don't know if he had to go to school over here. I know that in the commonwealth of Pennsylvania, all barbers are licensed. So there was probably some sort of exam, or work as an apprentice. He had his shop as part of his house, not far from us in Seward.

Jim: Did you visit often?

Shann: My brother and I truly grew up Italian. I remember we visited them every Sunday afternoon. I know that you being Italian would understand. That was the one day each week you would set aside to visit family. Grandpap wouldn't barber on Sunday.

Jim: Oh absolutely! That's right. Is your (maternal) grandmother still alive?

Shann: No, she passed away before my son was born in 1997, in the early winter. Now my dad's mother is still alive. She's 81, and still lives in the same house she's lived in since 1942. She lives there with my mother.

Jim: You're married? How many children do you have?

Shann: I've been married to Teresa for ten years, we have one boy, Devin. My son is four-and-a-half. He's an explorer, let's put it that way.

Jim: Does that mean he will make a good prospector.

Shann: Yes, actually he very much enjoys being in the dirt. I think he could possibly have a career as a geologist.

Jim: As a geologist or perhaps an engineer with earth-moving equipment. How about your grandparents on your father's side. Where did they come from?

Shann: Actually, one of my other relatives has traced my father's line all the way back to when they first arrived in the New World in 1701. The family name was originally Johns. His name was Griffith Johns from Wales. Now the little township where I grew up, called West Wheatfield Township, is where my father's family have been since the 1850s. This is actually a mildly funny point. My father's dad, Paul H. Jones, was the first one of the community to go even just one mile across the river to find a bride. It is really true that communities in Appalachia were very tightly knit back then. My father was actually the first one to leave the small valley or, as they said, "went over the hill" to find a bride. I was the first one to move out of state. I guess Devin will be the first one to leave the North American continent. I found that kind of interesting.

Jim: Tell us about your background in school.

Shann: I went to school in that town for a couple of years, and then the school district consolidated all of the elementary schools, and we went to school about ten miles away for elementary and secondary, which was seven through twelve.

Jim: Seven through twelve, that was junior and senior high combined.

Shann: Yes, combined. They didn't have enough kids to justify building two schools.

Jim: Did you play sports during high school?

Shann: I ran track for three years in junior high. I threw discus mainly, even lettered one year.

Jim: You didn't run in high school?

Shann: No.

Jim: Why not?

Shann: The competition got bigger, and I didn't.

Jim: What other sports did you play?

Shann: I wrestled from grade 7th to grade 11.

Jim: How did you do? Hold your own, most of the time?

Shann: Oh, I spent a fair amount of time counting the holes in the ceiling, if you know what I mean. I won a few matches. I did okay at 98 or 105, but when I got to 119, they were just too much for me. I remember one guy. We had a home and home match series with Blairsville, the neighboring district. When they came to our place, he didn't wipe me up—I know you've wrestled, and you've had this taste in your mouth—we drew.

Jim: You had a draw?

Shann: Yes, and we only drew because he had a penalty point against him. I didn't like how that match worked out.

Jim: You felt like you'd lost.

Shann: I didn't win in my own house. So, I found out that after the Christmas tournament this guy dropped a weight class. I was close to that weight class, and I really wanted a piece of this guy. So I sucked the weight down, and when we went to their place, I didn't pin him, but I wiped his nose on the mat for three periods.

Jim: That was your golden match?

Shann: Actually there was one other that no one expected me to win. The kid got stupid. He was wiping me across the mat through one period. He was up 5—1 after the first. Then in the second, I started down. I looked over at my coach, Bill Wilt, and my dad, who was his assistant, and they were signaling to me frantically to cradle this guy. By this time, I was sucking some serious wind. When the whistle blew, he started to ride me too high. So I reached over across my shoulders and cradled. Now this was our first home match that season. We had a packed gymnasium and I was the first wrestler. That place got real loud when I threw that guy on his back and pinned him.

Jim: Shouldn't have happened?

Shann: He wasn't a top-flight wrestler. A top-flight wrestler wouldn't have gotten that high.

Jim: I remember one time in my school, we had a meet with another school. I was wrestling 165 pounds, which is a weight class up from what I should have been...actually two weight classes up from what I should have been. We'd lost every match up to 165, and I saw the guy who was jumping around over there warming up, and he looked like a Greek god to me. Everybody was laughing when I stood up to warm up because I was so undersized compared to him. I felt a little bit intimidated by him and his size. The coach said, "Go do what you can." When I walked off the mat the coach said, "Madonna, you're an amazing wrestler." The guy never had a chance. He was on his back. I ran him around the mat. I did everything to him but pin him. That was the match, out of four years of wrestling, that sticks out in my mind as one of the most memorable. There were several others. Like you say, there are several matches. If you have 100 matches, there's always ten of them that stand out in your mind. Most of them were just matches. So I know what you mean when you say, "Yes there's one match." Beating the Greek god was my match. You also played other sports didn't you?

Shann: I played golf competitively for three years. I lettered for three years. It's not that I swung a very mean stick or that anyone was comparing me to Jack Nicklaus, but the way they had the rules set up, I always went out and got the points for my team. That was the name of the game. I went out there and beat my man in match play more times than not.

Jim: What did you do? Play against another person?

Shann: You played against another person. Okay, you had nine holes to a side. Now, it didn't matter if you won the hole by one stroke or ten, it only counted as one hole won. Whoever won the most holes on that side got a point for the team. Now, I would typically go out there and win four holes, push or draw two and lose three. On the three that I would lose, I'd blow up and shoot a real high score. That didn't matter as long as I won the side, 4—3. That was match play. Then you would get a point for the other nine holes, and then a third point for the most holes won on the total 18 holes.

Jim: I understand.

Shann: Usually I would turn my score card in. Coach would ask, "What did you shoot, Shann?" Ninety-eight, 102, sometimes even as high as 130. He'd shake his head in disappointment. Then he would ask, "How many points did you get, Shann?" Two-and-half I'd say. "Oh, good." As long as I beat the man, it didn't matter. The score counted, but only in case of a tie.

Jim: You're not big enough to have ever played football.

Shann: By the time I got to high school, Jim, the other boys were blowing right by me in size.

Jim: Like you said, you're only 5'4", 130 pounds. You didn't have the power. What did you do after high school?

Shann: I joined the Army a couple months after graduation.

Jim: What caused you to join the Army?

Shann: Lack of opportunities in the area at that time. In the early 1980s, the economy in western Pennsylvania, as well as the entire Ohio Valley, was rather depressed. Steel mills and coal mines were shutting down. Job opportunities weren't there. I wanted to go to school, but I wanted to foot my own bill for it.

Jim: Let me ask this question. You went into the service. Did you start at the bottom?

Shann: Buck private.

Jim: How far up did you go?

Shann: Made specialist, grade four, before I left.

Jim: What does that mean? How many steps was that?

Shann: Three additional steps.

Jim: How many years were you in the service?

Shann: Four active, two reserve.

Jim: All steps were in active?

Shann: Yes all steps were in active.

Jim: Is that about right for somebody in active?

Shann: Yes, for the job field I was in at the time.

Jim: What job field was that?

Shann: I was a photojournalist.

Jim: A photojournalist. That fits you. Tell us about that.

Shann: I did the basic training at Fort Knox, Kentucky. Most people don't enjoy that type of thing, but I did, to a large degree. My dad had a good point. He said, "Your drill sergeant can't possibly be as tough as your scoutmaster." He was right!

Jim: Was he your scoutmaster?

Shann: Oh no. My neighbor, Bill Bowers was my scoutmaster. The guy could yell and cuss. He had this deep booming voice that could fill the whole valley when it went off. He was a big man, and he loved his scouts.

Jim: And the scouts knew it?

Shann: Bill Bowers would do anything for us, and the five of us repaid him by achieving the rank of Eagle Scout. We were the first Eagle Scouts in the history of the troop.

Jim: Your drill sergeant wasn't as tough?

Shann: Oh Drill Sergeants Parker and Ramirez challenged us, but they were fair. The moving through the woods and staying in the field was old hat for me because I hunted and fished so much when I was a kid, and running around those hills was easy. I was in my element.

Jim: Were the packs as heavy as they say?

Shann: You know the only thing different between going up in the Brooks Range, and the field marches in the Army, is that there is no tripping over the tundra involved. The packs are still heavy.

Jim: I see, at least 90 pounds, right?

Shann: At least.

Jim: Following basic training, did you go into photojournalism right away?

Shann: Yes, I went to the Defense Information School near Indianapolis. I got the six-week crash course on how to use a single-lens reflex camera, process film and write stories and news releases. Originally I wanted to be a broadcaster, but they didn't have any slots available, so I got involved with the writing side.

Jim: Did you enjoy that?

Shann: Immensely. I was stationed at Fort Dix, New Jersey, as a low-rung journalist. I got to cover a lot of sports on post. I covered and wrote about training and maneuvers as well. Being the lowest ranking man, I drew most of the evening and weekend duty. Additionally, I still had to be ready for physical training at six a.m. At that time, all single solders had to do at least one year of overseas duty. A year went by and it was coming up to my turn. I had gotten reports from my friends that Korea was the last place on Earth I wanted to go. There was one person who used to be at Fort Dix who was reassigned to Alaska. He called me one day and said, "Look, there are some people up here leaving. You might want to put your name in because it's an overseas assignment." That sounded like a good idea, so I signed up. A couple months later orders came down for me to go to Alaska. I was due to be assigned to Fort Richardson (near Anchorage). I was scheduled to leave in May 1986. Well, the orders got changed. I wasn't to leave until September. In the meantime, I got transferred off of the _Fort Dix Post_ into the Outdoor Recreation Department to run the rifle range and skeet range for the summer. Finally I received a call saying that I was going to be assigned to Fort Greely, near Delta Junction. Everybody told me that Greely was the armpit of the universe and that I would hate it. I wondered what was so bad about Greely. Other soldiers who'd been there told me that the town only had a couple of thousand people. I was thinking to myself, "That's not much bigger than Robinson and Bolivar. How bad could it be? There's a major airport within 100 miles." So I came up to Fort Richardson, Alaska, in late September. That was okay. I flew to Fairbanks a few days later. The termination dust had fallen. I'd say I adapted pretty well. For anyone who wanted to get involved with that community, there was ample opportunity. Plus I had the opportunity that most 20-year-olds never get—I was the editor of the post newspaper. The only people I answered to were my shop sergeant, the post sergeant major, the deputy post commander and the post commander. If they told me to put it in the paper, I said, "Yes sir, three bags full." I got to cover a lot of different activities and events. For example, the Alaska Department of Fish and Game studied the bison herd near Delta Junction by radio collar. Now, because the herd also roams on the Army's land, Fish and Game got them to provide helicopter support to dart and collar some bison. I got to ride in the helicopter, shoot the photos and write the story.

Jim: Now that sounds like an interesting project. You single-handedly got to do all of the photography and write the story?

Shann: Yes, the story earned an Army-wide acclaim. I got an award out of that one.

Jim: Oh, what kind of award?

Shann: They called it a Fourth Estate Award for excellence in journalism. At the time I was stationed at Fort Greely, they did all of the cold weather testing. I got to go out with the people who did the testing, and do stories on different equipment and people. There was another group that did the mountain warfare training, repelling, glacier movements. We got to go out and photograph and be a part of all of those activities they were engaged in down by Black Rapids.

Jim: I've seen it. That was their mountain-climbing school, wasn't it?

Shann: The mountain-climbing school, exactly. Soldiers from all around the world would come there. The Chileans would come in and bring a liaison to work with them. They also had a mountain school in Chile where we'd occasionally send soldiers. We would have the Canadians at the Northern Warfare Training Center as well. As an aside, Black Rapids is where I had my actual first introduction to gold prospecting. There was a colonel down there at Black Rapids. He had a great assignment. He loved gold prospecting, and he wasn't too far from Gunnysack Creek. He was liking life that summer when I interviewed him. He told me he panned and sluice-boxed a lot of gold out of Gunnysack Creek.

Jim: Did you do anything other than journalism while you were in the service?

Shann: No that was it.

Jim: When did you get out?

Shann: I was out of the active duty in 1988 and out of the reserves in 1990.

Jim: What did you do when you got out of the Army in 1988?

Shann: I was engaged in some outdoor recreational pursuits in the fall of 1988. In January 1989, I began my education at the University of Alaska Fairbanks.

Jim: What kind of recreational pursuits where you involved in?

Shann: Let's see, I went on a caribou hunt, at the end of my service term, a moose hunt and a mountain goat hunt.

Jim: For your personal enjoyment. No journalism?

Shann: Yes, and then I went back to Pennsylvania to see my family for awhile.

Jim: How did you do on your hunts?

Shann: Moderately successful, broke some bones in my back.

Jim: You broke your back? You fell off the mountain?

Shann: I fell off the mountain.

Jim: Tell us that story.

Shann: Well, it's not as bad as it sounds. I had shot a caribou in mid-August up on Macomb Plateau, just outside of Delta Junction. We had boned out the meat, and we were packing it out. We were heading down-hill off the plateau, when I twisted my ankle in a washout in the trail. I just went tumbling down. I almost passed by my buddy on the way down. I got up, dusted myself off, and kept on trucking. About six weeks later, I couldn't quite get out of bed one morning. I went in and got an x-ray and theXXXXX's were broken. Those are the bones that stick out away from the spine. Those were what was cracked, not the bones that encase the spinal cord, but that would have explained why it hurt.

Jim: So what was the remedy for that. Bed-rest?

Shann: No, bed-rest made it worse. It was one of those things where you didn't feel like getting out of bed, but if you got up and walked about two miles, it loosened up enough where you could function. Every once in awhile it still hurts. I just take ibuprofen, get moving and start working—then it feels better.

Jim: I see. You started at the university in 1989. What discipline did you get involved with.

Shann: Secondary education.

Jim: You were going to be a schoolteacher. How long did that last?

Shann: One semester. I was disillusioned.

Jim: How were your grades?

Shann: Oh fine, I made the dean's list.

Jim: What did you do next?

Shann: I transferred into earth science.

Jim: That was in geology. How long did you stay with that?

Shann: I stayed with it for a year-and-a-half. Then I moved into mining engineering.

Jim: What in the world ever prompted you to move into mining engineering? The lure of gold?

Shann: Strangely enough, it wasn't gold.

Jim: I'm sure it couldn't have been coal.

Shann: No, it wasn't that black stuff either. For some reason, Jim, I was fascinated with putting holes in the ground.

Jim: Is that right. Pulling out chunks of ore of some kind.

Shann: Yes, and it had to be underground. Otherwise, it was not a real mine, at least not to me.

Jim: How did you do? Did you make the dean's list?

Shann: A couple of times.

Jim: Did you ever make the chancellor's list?

Shann: A couple of times.

Jim: Is that right, you made the chancellor's list. That is about as high as you can go. Did you get a degree?

Shann: Yes, I did.

Jim: What was your degree in?

Shann: In mining engineering. I graduated in 1999.

Jim: 1999. What took you so long? It took you ten years from the time you started college to the time you got your degree.

Shann: Well, I didn't go consecutively. I worked the whole time I was in school.

Jim: Tell us about the jobs you held as you worked your way through school.

Shann: I worked for awhile as a clerk for the Marine Sciences Department. I worked one summer as an engineering technician for Citigold Alaska. Then I got hooked up with the Mining Extension program.

Jim: What did you do there?

Shann: I was a lab and teaching assistant.

Jim: All-around handyman.

Shann: Whatever the boss needed done.

Jim: That was a good idea on your part. It could have been a short-lived job had you not been diversified. You worked for me from 1992—how long— about two, three years?

Shann: It was after I married Teresa in '92. I worked for you until '94. Then the position got eliminated. That last year we had one great year. We had over 300 students that year.

Jim: We had smooth sailing. Then they started scaling down the program.

Shann: Devaluing, I think would be a good term.

Jim: Well, what did you do in the meantime? Didn't you quit school for awhile?

Shann: Yes, for awhile. I was tired of going to school.

Jim: How long did you have to go to finish?

Shann: Oh, I don't even remember. It was less than a year, maybe less than a semester. Meanwhile, I worked at a hotel for awhile. Then in an appliance repair business for about three years.

Jim: What prompted you to go back to school?

Shann: A good buddy of mine drug me back kicking and screaming. He told me I really ought to get this unfinished business wrapped up.

Jim: I recall that. I said, "For goodness sake, Shann. You've only got four courses to go, and you're letting this degree slide away from you. Now let's get it done." So I acted as your co-advisor along with Paul Metz. We made certain everything got lined up, all letters and memos were written that would allow you to be reinstated and from then on everything was smooth sailing. Sometime during this period another event took place. Your son was born. When was that, Shann?

Shann: November 1997.

Jim: That was before you graduated. Did you go to work somewhere in the meantime?

Shann: At the time that I was thinking about going back to school. Mining Extension had been moved from the School of Mineral Engineering to

Alaska Cooperative Extension. With their new home came another opportunity to work for them.

Jim: In what capacity did you act?

Shann: Well, I was called an administrative assistant. In reality, it was the same capacity, as before—anything the boss needed done.

Jim: Administrative assistant was a good name for that position, but you also had the added responsibility as secretary. We graduated. Tell us about that.

Shann: That was a very good day! That rates right up there with completing basic training, because my best friend here retired Professor Emeritus, and I got my degree at the same time. That was just beautiful—poetic.

Jim: That's right. That was nice wasn't it, we walked away with our certificates in hand.

Shann: Exactly, and believe me, when I got that thing, I opened it up to make sure that diploma was indeed in there.

Jim: And it had your name on it.

Shann: Right.

Jim: We finished a period of our lives that was special, and we began to go off in somewhat different directions from the academic community as a teacher and student. You went to work at a couple of places after that. Oh, I remember, you stayed with Cooperative Extension.

Shann: That's right. I stayed with them for a year, but it wasn't the same. Now, you have to understand, I got to do things at Mining Extension not many students get an opportunity to do. After I proved some level of competency during my first stint, you came in and said, "Shann, I want you to do mine safety training. See what it takes to get it done." That was a great learning experience. Not many undergraduate students get the opportunity to work on course development. After I wrote everything out like you wanted it, you handed it back to me and said, "Here, teach it." Now, how many people get that opportunity?

Jim: That was in the first go-round. What about the second time you worked for me?

Shann: As well as shouldering the burden of being the Mining Extension secretary. I was also still a field and lab assistant, and I enjoyed accompanying you to the Brooks Range to do field work on geochemical prospecting. I learned a great deal there. That was absolutely one of the best experiences I ever had in Alaska.

Jim: Did you do anything else noteworthy while you were at Mining Extension?

Shann: Yes. In the second go-round, I have to give you credit for being innovative. I needed another course. So you set up an independent study with Paul Metz in the School of Mineral Engineering. Under your mentorship, I developed a rework of the Mining Extension Geophysical Prospecting course, which was a six-week introductory course in the geophysical methods a prospector uses to help find gold and other valuable metals in the ground. We took it all the way from the background through developing the course, a textbook and a workbook.

Jim: In fact you did write the textbook, and the workbook. As I recall I was on leave, and I was gone for a month-and-a-half. We conducted that work by correspondence, and I edited it, as you taught it. That was 1999.

Shann: That was a good course.

Jim: That was a very good course.

Shann: It was a good program all around. After graduation I spent another year with Extension. After the Cooperative Extension director decided he was going to take another direction with that program, I transferred to the UAF Geophysical Institute, where I work today.

Jim: That was superlative work we did in the Brooks Range on geochemical prospecting. With the background you have in geophysical prospecting it put you in a prime position to say, "I may not have all of the skills in the field, but I know the theory and I have had the experience of applying it in the field." You could probably also say, "I have the background in both geochemistry and geophysics to run an exploration program properly. I did geochemistry in the Brooks Range, and I did the geophysics in the Tanana-Yukon uplands and the Fairbanks Mining District." You have a good solid background in both exploration methods. Tell us a little bit more about what you got out of Mining Extension.

Shann: Using mineral evaluation as an example: The students and I systematically collected samples from a mining property and then crushed, ground, pulverized, sieved and tabled those samples. Ultimately they were tested by simple chemical field tests while other portions of the samples were prepared to be sent off to an analytical laboratory for in-depth analysis. We then interpreted those results and determined whether or not the property was worth developing.

Jim: If I recall correctly you earned the two-year Mineral Exploration and Mining Technology Certificate from Mining Extension. Those Mining Extension courses provided the application of theory that the mining engineering courses gave you. Did you go to field camp?

Shann: I didn't have to for my mining engineering degree. However, I did more field work than other mining engineering students as I satisfied the requirements for the Mining Extension two-year certificate.

Jim: Every Mining Extension course had 25 to 40 percent laboratory or field work associated with it.

Shann: Not only for the courses I took, but all of the courses I was the teaching assistant for and some of the field research that Mining Extension did. You always said that a person learns more by teaching the course than they ever did by taking the course, and they learn more by doing the actual application in the field than they could just listening to the theory. So if they apply it, they learn it—do it physically with their hands. If the student looks at the result of his or her work, they will understand what is going on much better than just listening to the theory. Now, I took that Mining Extension model and used it to develop a one-credit fly-fishing course offered through UAF Summer Sessions. Fly-fishing is one of my true loves. For the last quarter century, I have worked to perfect this craft that my father spent many hours teaching me. This past winter, I started to formulate this dream, similar to a program offered at Pennsylvania State University and Montana State University. Having the background in course development from Mining Extension, under your direction, I was able to know how to structure a practical course that is geared for intellectual growth. I didn't want to rebuild the wheel. So I got with the other universities that offer similar programs, and they sent their outlines and other course development materials. I had good contacts from Auburn University, Penn State, Montana State and the University of Virginia. I got feedback from these schools to make sure that I was hitting all of the major points. Then, I took part of what I wanted to cover in the one-credit class and offered it as a Fairbanks Community Schools short course. That was very well received. I made changes based on what I learned at Community Schools, for the one-credit class. Like you said, Jim, you learn more from teaching the course. How can I change it here? How can I make it better?

Jim: You bring up two points here, Shann. The first point is you're learning how to teach by teaching the course, because you can see the holes in the style. So you plug them up. The other one is that you learn to refine your technique because you're having to explain it in more detail than when you are out there doing it. Sometimes in the field alone you don't think about why you are doing something a certain way. Teaching forces you to analyze why you do something and present it clearly to the students. Often times, you don't know why you have developed certain techniques until you analyze them for your students—probably because you've been doing it forever.

Shann: That's exactly right. Things that you think of as second nature, a student is always going to put a new set of eyes on, and ask you those questions. I tell my students, "It's okay to challenge me with your questions." In developing the course, in some respects, this year, I became a better angler, because I had to analyze and refine techniques I don't normally use.

Jim: I don't know that you're such a hot angler. I've never seen you come through my door with a fish for me.

Shann: Now do I have to tell everybody about Baby Creek?

Jim: That was a funny story. Okay, tell your story about Baby Creek in the Brooks Range.

Shann: Jim and I and his dogs flew into Chandalar Lake in Jim's Cessna 206, took a portable inflatable rubber boat about ten miles up the Chandalar River to the mouth of Baby Creek. There we had set up the tent after we had boated all night. The next morning we could hear wolves howling. Now this was late morning. Jim's smaller dog, Cindy, was looking and barking at something that I thought was across the river. I thought it could be a wolf, and I really didn't want to get involved with that. She kept staring across the river. I was trying to figure what she was looking at over there, because the brush over there wasn't taller than waist high. Finally, I looked down into the stream, and there was this huge Arctic grayling. That thing was 20 inches-plus, as sure as I am sitting here. It was stuck in the low current. Your mantra in the field is "more food is better," so I scoop up this fish. I ran it over to the tent. I caught it in my bare hand, and its trying to squirm away. "Hey, Jim, you want fish for breakfast?"

Jim: That was a big fish. I have to admit it was a specimen. An angler would have enjoyed catching that on a hook, but catching it with your bare hands trapped in the shallows, that was interesting too.

Shann: But your dog pointing it out was the more intriguing part. That was teamwork.

Jim: Shann, I would like to jump back to one little item here. During your time as a student at the University of Alaska, I'm sure that you were exposed to the history of Alaska, drift mining, gold mining, historical gold mining, things of that type. You've probably read a few papers on it. Are you familiar with the drift-mining method?

Shann: Yes, I have read extensively on the old drift-mining practices.

Jim: Did you get this through your professional degree?

Shann: No, we only had one course that covered historical mining practices. I got most of my knowledge on early placer mining from my work at the Mining Extension service. Not only were there a lot of papers there, they had an extensive library.

Jim: Oh, you learned about drift mining there. As I recall too, I gave a lot of drift mining in the classes, and handed out professional papers. Parker also had one. Did you read Parker's paper? She had a good presentation I thought.

Shann: Yes I read her thesis. I thought it was very well done.

Jim: This is one of the reasons I wanted to talk to you. I thought you might be willing to help me out on the presentation of Felix Pedro's life, which I will be writing in the near future, and we'll get back to you on that. Is there anything else coming up that's new and exciting?

Shann: Well the 100th anniversary of Felix Pedro's gold discovery. There will be many events that I have been asked to attend.

Jim: They are going on all week this week, and we hope to have you involved in a roundtable discussion on Felix Pedro's life.

Shann: That will be interesting. I look forward to that.

Jim: Thank you for the interview, Shann.

Shann: It has been a pleasure, Jim.

Massimo Turchi
with
Jim Madonna

In Fanano, Italy
April 2001

Jim: On our traveling interview segment we are in Fanano, Italy, the birthplace of Felix Pedro, known here as Felice Pedroni. Massimo Turchi, the director of tourism for the region, is going to give us an overview of his life in the region. Massimo is also going to tell us about the closing chapters of Felix Pedro and the monuments and activities that are preserved in Fanano in his honor. Massimo, give us some of your background. Where were you born?

Massimo: I was born in Fanano in 1972.

Jim: You're 39 years old.

Massimo: Yes.

Jim: Did you have a lot of brothers and sisters? That seems to be the trend—big families.

Massimo: Believe it, I was the only child.

Jim: It is hard for me to believe, but I will try. Did you go to school in Fanano?

Massimo: Yes, I went to primary school in Fanano. Afterwards, I went for my secondary education in Cabulo, located about 35 kilometers south of here.

Jim: What kind of work do you do?

Massimo: I work in tourism. I divide up my work in the area of North Apennine of Modena. We work to increase our tourism—attract more people. We have a lot of activities such as football, cycling, and we are developing a program for children in mountain orientation. We are also developing a little park for adults where we will have a display of a rocker box and sluice box and I will act out the role of Felix Pedro discovering gold in Alaska, on the day of the festivities.

Jim: Perhaps you wouldn't mind taking a few pictures of the park and festivities and sending them to us. It may make a good story for our newspaper.

Massimo: Oh yes, definitely.

Jim: When did you start studying the life of Felix Pedro?

Massimo: I started studying about Felix Pedro ten years ago.

Jim: Do you know Felix Pedro's family?

Massimo: Yes, one of his distant relatives, John Franco Pedroni, knew a lot about Felix. When his father was a young boy he knew Felix and he told John Franco many stories about Felix's adventures in Alaska.

Jim: And that is where you got most of your information about Felix and his discovery of gold in Alaska?

Massimo: Yes, and from the University of Alaska library.

Jim: When you come to Alaska during the centennial celebration we want to invite you to share all the details at a roundtable discussion of Felix Pedro's life. We can weave what you have on the life of Felix Pedro and the discovery of gold in Alaska with that of a few other people and see if we can't come up with a fairly accurate description of the events that led up to the founding of Fairbanks and the role that Felix Pedro's discovery of gold in the Tanana Valley played.

Massimo: I will look forward to it, Jim.

Jim: Thank you for the interview, Massimo.

Massimo: I enjoyed it, and we of Fanano are pleased that you visited us.

The Life of
Felix Pedro
(1858-1910)

Photograph courtesy of University of Alaska Archives.

Introduction

Imagine a hypothetical situation, if you will, a house nestled in spruce and birch trees high on a ridge near Fairbanks, Alaska. Now imagine a rectangular room in this house; the walls are a red-beige color. At one end of this room is a large picture window that overlooks the Tanana Valley. In the foreground, far below, you can see the Chena River as it threads its way serpent-like from its headwaters in the Yukon-Tanana Uplands to the Tanana Flats below. There you can see the mouth of the little river as it empties into the larger, braided Tanana River that has its source in the Alaska Range to the south-east. Above the confluence of the two streams you can make out Bates Rapids, the shallows that prevented many early-time paddle wheel riverboats from traveling farther into the Interior drained by the Tanana. Farther to the north-east you can see the city of Fairbanks and in the distance to the south-east you can see the Alaska Range. All this is in a setting of thick, green spruce, aspen and birch trees.

The beige walls of the room are decorated with pictures and maps—maps of the Tanana Valley goldfields in the early part of the gold rush, pictures of riverboats, old Fairbanks, and most important, independent pictures of the three men who played the most important roles in the founding of Fairbanks—E.T. Barnette, Judge James Wickersham and Felix Pedro. In the center of the room is a round table with an assortment of reference books and papers on the discovery of gold in 1902 and the history of Fairbanks. Sitting around that table are five people. I am fortunate to be one of those people. To my left is Massimo Turchi from Fanano, Italy. Next to Massimo is Shann Jones, a mining engineer who graduated from the University of Alaska. Next to Shann is Terrence Cole, history professor at the University of Alaska Fairbanks and author of *Crooked Past,* The history of early Fairbanks. Next to Terrence and to my right is Johne Binkley, riverboat captain and third-generation Alaskan. My name is Jim Madonna. The date is July 22, 2002—the centennial anniversary of the discovery of gold in the Tanana Valley. The subject we are discussing is the life of the man who made that first gold discovery—**Felix Pedro.**

Felix Pedro (Felice Pedroni)

Jim: Alaska Gold Trails has led us into some strange territory here—the mid 1800s. I am uncertain whether to start with the early methods of prospecting and drift mining in the frozen ground of Canada and Alaska or whether to begin with Felix Pedro. Regardless, I want to thank the four of you for providing the interviews. It would be impossible to put this together without your help. Let's start with the early days of Felix Pedro's life. Massimo, give us some background on Felix—when was he born?

Massimo: He was born April 18, 1858, to Giuseppe and Carolina Pedroni in the little village of Trignano di Fanano in the Province of Modena, Italy. Trignano is a small village in the municipality of Fanano, but Felix was raised in a house called Tegge on the outskirts of the village, not in the center. He was the fourth of six children—three brothers and two sisters. He was born Felice Pedroni. He did not become known as Felix Pedro until he arrived in the United States.

Jim: The literature has some discrepancies regarding the life of Felix Pedro. One of them was his age. Some sources have his birth year set at 1860, others at 1858 and still others at 1859. There are several formal documents that indicate that 1858, as you suggested, is the correct one.

Massimo: Memories fade. Most of my information is provided by the living members of the Pedroni family, Philip Lelli (family historian) and various book and newspaper articles, such as the one translated into English by Professor Angelo Pellegrini. Also, the book by Donna Salter Mullen regarding the Pedroni family is the most accurate account of the family tree. All this information is fairly accurate regarding Felice's life before he left for the United States, but maybe not so much after he left Italy. I am anxious to hear the results of the historic research on Felice after he arrived in America.

Jim: What type of environment existed in the area where Felix was born and raised, and what were the social conditions that existed there?

Massimo: When Felice was born, Trignano was a small village of several hundred people. It is located in the north-central Apennines at an elevation of about 2000 feet. The climate, which is typical of the mountainous region, is very cold in the winter too mildly warm in the summer. Several mountains rise high above the community, the highest of which is Mount Cimone, which is over 7000 feet. This is the physical environment Felice was born into. Socially, he was born into a very poor working-class family in which every member of the family even the children at the youngest age had to work hard to make a living. Felice's father, like many of the men of the area would work in the Fanano area near his home in the summer, then in the winter migrate to larger towns and cities like Tuscany where he would work for pitiful wages to supplement his family's livelihood. In Trignano, Felice's father was a woodcutter, making charcoal out of the wood. The family also raised goats, sheep and other livestock. In the winter he would migrate to the plains where he would find employment as a sheepherder (a shepherd). I would say that although the physical environment was a challenging one for an adventurous boy like Felice, his social environment was one of poverty. This was the humble social environment that Felice was raised in, and in this environment formal education was not available. As a consequence Felice never learned to read or write, but much good came from it. Felice learned how to work and work hard. He learned how to concentrate on the task at hand and never waver from his goal. From his early years he showed a preference for being alone and, some say, living dangerously. He was a strong, well-muscled young man with broad shoulders, and stood about 5-feet 9-inches tall—a little above average for his time. He often hunted the fox and the rabbit that lived among the chestnut trees of the area. As a result he became an excellent marksman. His adventurous and inquisitive nature sent him hiking in the mountains even to the snow-covered summit of Mount Cimone.

Jim: Seemingly it was Felix's adventurous spirit, physical strength and acquired skills developed during his impoverished youthful years that would work in harmony to direct his life. What kind of work did he do when he was young, Massimo?

Massimo: Like all of the Pedroni children, Felix went to work at a young age. It was natural for him to follow his father's guidance. He first started out by cutting the wood, then later, like his father, he began herding the cattle and the sheep. He rode a horse; he was like a cowboy. As you indicated, both woodcutting and riding and his familiarity with horses were skills he would later use in Alaska. Although all the children of the Pedroni family worked, life was a struggle in Trignano. It seemed that it could get no worse, but it did when Felice's father, Giusseppi, died unexpectedly. The burden of raising the children, who at that time ranged in age between eight and seventeen, then shifted to Felix's mother, Carolina. Felix was 13 years old at that time. Soon after that the family began to disunite. The oldest brother left for Sardinia while two others joined the mass of Italians immigrating to the United States. Several years after his father's death, Felice traveled to France. He worked in the coal mines of France until he was 21. Then he returned to Trignano, where he began courting a young woman. The story goes that Felice was not a calm man. He attended a dance one evening which almost ended in tragedy. Another young man engaged Felice in an argument. The young men moved out into the courtyard. Apparently there was a lot of yelling and screaming, perhaps a struggle, and finally the sound of a rifle shot. It is unknown who exactly fired the rifle. It was soon learned, however, that the quarrel was about the dark-haired girl Felice was attempting to court, which was contested by the other. The matter inflamed several members of the community, and the young girl finally repulsed him. Ultimately, life in Fanano became difficult for Felice, and with a broken heart, at the age of 23, he left Italy for the United States.

Jim: What year was that, and which port did Felix leave from?

Massimo: He left Italy from the port at Genoa, and he landed in New York in 1881. He was 23 years old. From the East Coast he worked his way west on the railroad. Finally he ended up in Washington, where he went to work in the coal mines.

Jim: Yes, the way I understand it from the literature, he first went to work for the railroad in Peoria, Illinois, as a section hand. He lived with a relative in Peoria. Unfortunately, there was no reference that I encountered indicating the relationship. We know that two of his older brothers left for the United States a few years before Felix, but the documents and articles that I have surveyed did not indicate if it was his brother that he stayed with. Regardless, the newspaper articles (Lelli), historical reports (Pellegrini), books (Wickersham) and many other articles suggest that Felix worked for the railroad for about two years before moving west.

Massimo: Yes, now I recall. He worked in the silver, gold and coal mines in Colorado and Utah to earn the money to continue his trip westward. It took three years from the time he left Peoria to reach the West Coast. He arrived in Jacksonville, Oregon, in the summer of 1886. He then migrated northward to Washington, where he went to work in the coal mines at Franklin and Carbonado.

Jim: The sense I perceive is that he spent most of his time at the Carbonado mines, but in general, due largely to his restless, adventurous and energetic nature, he never stayed in one place very long. It was while he was working in the Carbonado mines that he met his best friends, among them, his greatest benefactor, August Hanot, Sr. It was in the Hanot home that he met other Italian immigrants who would play an important role in his future. Among them were Stefano Absena and the Costa brothers, Giovonni and Francesco. It wasn't long before the four men accompanied by Lewis Jones whom, according to Pelligrini, Felix had met in Franklin in 1888, made plans to search for gold in the Cariboo country of Canada. Apparently Felix was extremely well trusted by Hanot, because it was Hanot that grubstaked him for the trip, and in the spring of 1892 the five men arrived in the Cariboo. Felix remained in the Cariboo for almost a year before he realized that his first search for gold had failed.

Massimo: He returned to Washington in 1883, where some say he went to work in the Carbonado coal mines, while others say he never returned to coal mining.

Jim: Yes, I found that confusing as well. Regardless, he continued to spend a lot of time in the Hanot home enjoying his favorite pastime of listening to adventure stories and telling his own. Perhaps it would be appropriate to add here that it was the Cariboo adventure that sparked Felix Pedro's spirit regarding the search for gold, and he was eager to hear any stories regarding gold discoveries and mining in a frontier environment.

Massimo: He was definitely prepared for the next fellow he would meet. It was in the Hanot home that he met a fellow Italian by the name of Espalmer. Espalmer was one of the frontiersmen who had for several years made a living mining gold in the gold-rich Fortymile area of Alaska. Felix loved listening to his stories. The spark of interest in gold mining burst into a flame, and it wasn't long before they began making plans to go to the Fortymile country. In February of 1894 a group of five men including Espalmer, the Costa brothers, Absena and Felix Pedro began the trip into the Fortymile.

Jim: It is important to note that August Hanot, Sr. had such faith in Felix that he once again financed his trip. Some areas of confusion arose surrounding the trip. I have not come across any literature that describes the journey to the Interior of Alaska. Wharton, in his book *The Alaskan Goldrush,* made mention that Felix and, I presume, the entire Espalmer party, went by ship through the Inside Passage to Juneau, then onward to Dyea where they crossed the Chilkoot pass. The Chilkoot pass by the way, was first used as a route by the prospectors and trappers in 1885, when a fellow by the name of Holt first established it as one of the most favorable routes to the Interior. As far as the Espalmer party goes, it was probably in March of 1894 that they ascended the pass and made their way down to the headwaters of Lake Bennett. Now the question becomes, did they build a boat and wait until the spring thaw brought the water to float down the Yukon River, or did they travel over the frozen river to the Fortymile Area? Seemingly, the dangers of the Chilkoot and building a boat at Lake Bennett then floating from the headwaters of the Yukon to the Fortymile through all the dangerous rapids would have been an experience that would have found its way into the literature. In addition, if they had gone down the surface of the frozen river, many questions come to mind. Did they pack their provisions, or did they have dog teams, or did they use sleds that they pulled? Regardless, if they went over the frozen surface of the Yukon River there must have been some stories worth mentioning. We have to keep in mind that Felix's main social addiction was to sit around and listen to or tell stories. Yet there is a big historical vacancy between the time they crossed the Chilkoot Pass and the time Felix arrived in the Fortmile; there doesn't seem to be anything in the literature that describes the adventure of the Espalmer party from the Chilkoot Pass to the Fortymile. Have any of you heard, or do you know how Felix traveled to the Fortymile in 1894?

Johne: That's right. There should have been some record or story about that trip, but I haven't heard of any.

Jim: Unless there is something hidden away in the archives that we don't know about, it seems like there was about 18 months of Felix's history missing—the first of two 18-month mysteries. The next we hear of Felix is that he is in the Fortymile in the summer and fall of 1895. The general statement was that there were several ways he could earn a grubstake in Alaska at that time such as working for a gold miner, cutting cordwood for the riverboats, or being grubstaked by one of the traders. Felix's activities were reported in the 1909 edition of *Alaska-Yukon Magazine,* which indicated that his first stop in Alaska was in the Fortymile country, where he prospected and mined gold. It is likely that although the report stated that he was working in the Fortymile area in 1895, since he began his trip in March of 1894 he more than likely arrived in the Fortymile in the summer or fall of that year (1894). This is where he began learning the method of prospecting and mining for flood-gold— the gold that is fine enough to occupy the surface of the gravels. It is likely that his first teacher was Espalmer. Regardless, it was a time of education for Felix. The timing was perfect, not only for Felix's education but for the education of all the miners in the north country at that time. Let me first provide a little background. Placer mining in Interior Alaska had a very interesting beginning. As early as 1885, John Manook discovered placer gold in the Rampart District. Then later, Pitka and Soresco discovered gold on Birch Creek just out of Circle, and it was that discovery that stabilized Circle City as a trading post on the Yukon River. Now the interesting part about all of this was presented in Ogilvie's book, *Early Days on the Yukon.* He describes what mining was like prior to 1890. In that time all the placer mining was done for skim gold or flood gold. The basic deposition of placer gold deserves explaining. Deposit-wise, there are two end results to placer gold deposition—one is flood gold, and the other is paystreak gold. Flood gold is that gold that is small enough and fine enough to be carried along by the mechanical energy of the stream and become deposited among the first two or three inches of gravel along gravel bars during periods of low water, only to remain there until the next flood stage, when it will be picked up and carried on down to the next river bar or dropped when the mechanical energy of the water decreases. It is not hard to imagine how flood gold can be carried miles away from the source area. Paystreak gold, on the other hand, is that gold that makes its way down through the stream gravels and ultimately finds its way to the interface of the gravels and the bedrock below, thereby providing an elongated depositional pattern on bedrock. Paystreak gold is commonly much richer than is flood gold and the larger, more valuable deposits generally form near the source area. Strangely, the presence of flood gold does not always indicate a valuable paystreak below, and conversely, the absence of significant flood gold does not always indicate the absence of a valuable paystreak below.

Shann: Ogilvie found, during his wanderings back in the late 1800s, that on the Stewart River and other northland streams the riverbars were extremely rich. In some cases—the Stewart River being the prime example—they were capable of extracting as much as $100 a day in gold off the river bars. Now this was the same thing that John Manook and Soresco were doing in the Interior of Alaska—mining flood gold. It wasn't until 1895 that the miners began perfecting the methods of drift mining.

Jim: Exactly. In fact it was at that same period of time that Felix Pedro came into the country. He was in the Fortymile when the miners had their first meeting. It could be suggested that it was the first miner's conference in Alaska. According to Ogilvie, the miners got together on several occasions following that first conference and discussed the different methods of mining, including the different methods of thawing frozen ground and drift mining. So it is with Ogilvie's presentation on that first 1895 meeting that we have historical information regarding advancements in drift mining technology. The fact that Felix Pedro was in the country suggests that he was on the cutting edge of new prospecting and mining techniques. Felix was a good listener, and it is probable that he learned a great deal from these conferences and the men who attended them.

Johne: That is an interesting bit of information. I have often wondered how drift mining was first developed in the frozen ground of Alaska.

Jim: Ogilvie's book provided a great deal of beneficial background information. Unfortunately there was no reference, that I could find, regarding Pedro, nor did he expand on the different methods of prospecting and mining frozen ground and their purposes. Shann, you probably have had experience, as a student of mining at the University of Alaska, with mining frozen ground in Alaska. Do you have something along these lines you can share with us?

Shann: Yes. Following the miners' meetings, the early-day Alaska and Yukon prospectors and miners continued to look for flood gold on small streams, as the indicator of valuable deposits. When they found fair prospects they would engage in one of three main methods of mining activity in the frozen ground. One was the prospect shaft, the second was open-cut mining, and the third method was drift mining. The purpose of a prospect shaft was to determine the depth to bedrock, if there was gold disseminated among the gravels from the surface down, and if there was a valuable paystreak at or near bedrock—in general, to evaluate the ground. If the ground was valuable enough to mine, the miners would then decide on which of two mining methods to use. Where the gold-bearing gravels were less than ten feet thick they would use the open-cut method. If the frozen gravels were thicker, and suitable for tunneling (drifting) along the interface of the gravels and bedrock, it became more desirable to use the drift mining method.

Jim: Can you give us some background on open-cut placer mining?

Shann: Sure. In early-day open-cut mines, the paystreak gravels lay within six to ten feet of the surface. Often times all of the mining-related activity would take place during the summer or ice-free season. They would open up ground—remove vegetation and upper few inches of soil in the early spring, thereby allowing the warmer days of summer to thaw the gravel—then they would mine it and process the gold-bearing gravels as they thawed and before the winter freeze-up brought activity to a halt. In the earliest days this was all done by hand. The material was loosened by means of pick and shovel, and transported by wheelbarrows to the head of a wooden sluice, where running water washed the gold from the gravels into riffles. This method was only good for rich, shallow deposits; otherwise the early hand methods just didn't pay. Often, on the same small creek, in the upper limits where the frozen ground was shallow, they would open-cut mine, and lower in the valley, where the ground was deeper, they would drift mine the deposit by dropping a shaft through the frozen gravel to the bedrock below, then radiating out with drifts, like spokes on a wheel, in search of the valuable paystreak.

Johne: How did they manage to produce a shaft in solidly frozen ground out in the wilderness, back in the early days, without the aid of sophisticated equipment?

Shann: As you pointed out Johne, the gold-bearing gravels of this area were frozen solid. As a result early miners found it necessary to thaw the ground to develop a prospect shaft down to bedrock. This was accomplished by setting a wood fire over a selected area. The fire would thaw six to eight inches of frozen gravel. The miner would muck out the thawed ground then reset a pile of firewood to repeat the process.

Gradually, by repeating the cycle, he would develop a shaft approximately four feet by four feet that extended to bedrock. Once the miner got down a few feet to where he could no longer shovel the material out of the shaft over his head or haul the material up by hand, he would construct what is called a "windlass," similar to the hoisting device used in old-time, open, water wells to crank a rope around a spool to raise a bucket of water, but in this case they would hoist the gold-bearing gravels from the depth of the shaft to the surface. Once on the surface, the gold-bearing gravels were dumped into stockpiles to await the spring thaw, which brought the water for sluicing. I should add that it was this, and techniques like this, that Felix Pedro learned at these miners meetings and from the men who had the experiences.

Jim: I heard somewhere that as they went down deeper with their shaft, that at a certain point they would run out of oxygen to keep the fire burning.

Shann: Yes. In deeper shafts they hung a piece of canvas called a "Brattice cloth" down the center of the shaft that would create a natural air draw or convection—warm, oxygen-depleted, smoke-filled air would rise on one side of the cloth, as cool, oxygen-rich air was drawn down on the other, thereby keeping the fire burning.

Terrence: I have a two-part question on the historical development of drift mining that is a puzzle: First, were the early prospectors dropping the shafts during the winter in the existing stream channel? Second, how did the prospectors and miners of the early 1890s first recognize that valuable paystreaks existed beneath ten feet or more of solidly frozen river gravels?

Jim: Those are good questions. Let me attempt an answer, Terrence. The answer to your first question is that a stream meanders, with time, back and forth across its channel, and if it is draining a gold-bearing area it will create paystreaks as it meanders. The prospectors would drop their prospect shafts generally in the winter because the opening would re-main frozen and stable. The shaft would be positioned off to the side of the existing stream in a location that looked most promising. The an-swer to your second question is a little more complex. Actually mining flood gold from the upper few inches of riverbar gravels was probably the precursor to open-cut mining, and open-cut mining was probably the precursor to drift mining. The way I understand it is that in the early days, when the miners were mining strictly flood gold, which usually occupied the first few inches of gravel on a river bar, they sometimes found that the gold was disseminated throughout the gravel all the way down to bedrock. In the shallower gravels they would mine the entire depth. Occasionally, especially where the deposit was fairly close to the hard-rock source of the placer gold, they would find a large increase in gold concentration and larger nuggets at the bedrock-gravel interface. They would continue to follow this enriched zone, which generally presented itself as an elongate somewhat serpent-like pattern down the older abandoned river channel. As they open-cut mined the deposit down the channel, the thickness of the frozen gravel increased, and as these thicknesses increased to greater than ten or more feet it became easier to drive a drift along the bedrock-gravel interface than mine the entire thickness of gravel, which in the thicker deposits commonly become much leaner and unprofitable to mine. They then would leapfrog down the stream channel, dropping shafts to intercept the paystreak, then drift back along the paystreak, thereby interconnecting with the previous shaft. In addition they would drift down the channel from each shaft until it was more convenient and economical to drop another shaft. With this early knowledge came the concept of dropping a prospect shaft in search of valuable gold deposits hidden beneath dozens of feet of frozen gravel. These were all valuable methods that Felix Pedro learned when he first entered the Fortymile area in 1895. He used these techniques later in his personal search for gold. Felix soon became widely known as a meticulous prospector and expert miner.

Johne: Didn't Felix go to the Klondike during that gold rush?

Jim: Yes he did, Johne. Felix was in the Fortymile in August, 1896, when news came that George Washington Carmack had discovered gold in the Klondike, according to an Angello Pellagrini translation found in the UAF archives. It should be kept in mind that no one outside of the Yukon and Alaska knew of the strike in the Yukon at that time, and Felix Pedro had an opportunity to be among the first prospectors to enter the Klondike River area and prospect its gold-rich tributaries. Indeed, his inquisitive nature drove him to visit and inspect the area along with the majority of prospectors from Circle and Fortymile. He could have easily staked a rich claim, but there was something inside him that left him discontent with the thought. There were too many people in the new region to suit him. He stayed only three months. This event probably more than any other in his life provided the clarity of Felix Pedro's character. At heart, Felix Pedro was not a miner, he was a prospector and an adventurer. It was always the lure of new country and the thrill of discovery that drove Felix. Several years later Wickersham, in his book *Old Yukon,* would describe Pedro as "slender, alert, erect, clear-eyed and at home in wilderness or mining camp." Furthermore it was suggested in the May 1903 edition of *The Fairbanks Miner* that "his stories regarding his long summer tours afoot, his dangerous encounters with aggressive grizzlies and bull moose, the times he was eaten by the ferocious and unrelenting Alaskan mosquitoes, and how he had to eat his dogs to survive, were just a few of the hardships Felix experienced as he traveled through deep, wooded valleys and over the high, snow-covered passes of the Alaska Range, always in search of that one precious discovery that would quench the fire in his soul—GOLD."

Shann: It is strange that he would not have taken advantage of the Klondike discovery like so many others did.

Jim: It does seem strange doesn't it, but it was this passion for prospecting and adventure, in 1898, while others from around the world were scurrying across the routes to the Klondike, that Felix and his partner A.C. Canning, a young engineer, took another direction, which led Felix into the Tanana Valley for the first time. In the early spring of the year they took their outfit up the Fortymile then crossed the Yukon-Tanana Uplands to the Tanana River where, after breakup of ice on the river, they built a boat and prospected the streams entering the Tanana. They found their best prospects in the Salcha River drainage. It was in a branch of the Salcha that they discovered a large quartz vein. Canning examined the vein while Felix panned the gravels of the stream, which according to his experience, "was one of the richest creeks he had ever prospected." Although Pedro would have liked to remain, winter was coming on and the two men were low on food; they were forced to begin the long trek over the Yukon-Tanana Uplands to Fortymile. But before leaving, Pedro fixed several markers in his mind—the junction of the two streams, an Indian village, the location of the boat that they cached along with a portion of their outfit at the headwaters of the stream, and naturally the white-quartz vein. As they made the trek back toward the Fortymile the men began to run out of food, the winter weather began to set in, and they became disoriented in the uncharted wilderness of Interior Alaska. They began the struggle for survival. Out of food and exposed to the elements, the two men made their way through the wilderness, over the mountains and, through shear determination, into Fortymile. Some say that it was that discovery of gold that, like a magnet, kept attracting Felix Pedro back into the Tanana Valley in search of what became known as "Lost Creek."

Terrence: Yes, that is the way I understood it. For two years after this experience, Pedro worked in the Circle City mines to earn enough for an outfit.

Shann: I understood that he might have also earned money cutting wood for the riverboats. By the way, were those the placer mines located on Birch and Faith Creeks?

Terrence: Yes. Whenever he had earned enough to assemble an outfit he would head back into the hills. He walked hundreds of miles between the Chatanika River and the Goodpaster River, always in search of the "Lost Creek." I believe he took two full trips into the area. Many of his friends began to doubt whether it had ever existed.

Shann: Perhaps it was his final trip...the dates are somewhat vague, but I think it was in 1899 that he ran into Alfred Brooks of the U.S. Geological Survey. Does anyone know the background on that particular meeting?

Massimo: Yes. As you might guess, traveling all those hundreds of miles on foot wore out Felix's shoes. The way I understand the story, he killed a bear and made mukluks or moccasins out of its hide. He was very satisfied with his new footwear although they were not as adequate as a pair of boots. As he continued his prospecting he was spotted by members of the Brooks party, which was surveying the geology and geography of the area. When Brooks saw Felix's moccasins he right away invited him to the camp and supplied him with a pair of sturdy rubber-soled boots. Felix worked for Brooks as a packer and prospector, and it was during this time that the two men shared information. His time working for Brooks, and the new information he gathered, helped Felix become more familiar with the land, and he was more certain than ever that he would make a valuable discovery in the Tanana area. Before he could pursue his dream he had to return to Circle for supplies. One account suggested that he went back to work in the placer mines of Birch Creek to acquire the funds for an outfit.

Johne: I came across that same account. It was also suggested that he might have returned to the most reliable of all methods of earning money, and that was cutting wood for the steamboats, which were beginning to travel the Yukon in larger and larger numbers in response to the Klondike strike and stampede.

Jim: Seemingly, like you said Johne, when a prospector was in need of a grubstake he could always turn to cutting wood. I don't know where I read it, but one account suggested that almost every prospector along the shores of the Yukon cut wood for the steamboats at one time or another. I don't know how true that was, but there were a lot of cases where the truth was stretched a bit, and sometimes there were simply inaccuracies in relating information. For example there were a number of conflicting accounts during the period of time between 1898, when Pedro first discovered gold in "Lost Creek" and 1902, when he made his discovery on Pedro Creek. All of them seem to contain some useful information. Terrence, when you did your research what did you come up with as the most plausible event that followed Pedro's work with Brooks?

Terrence: Well Jim, like you said, there were a number of conflicting accounts, and not just during the period we are talking about here, but all through Pedro's life, from the year he was born all the way through to who he was with during some of his excursions into the Tanana Valley. Like you said, he made at least two trips into the area during the two years following his discovery of gold on "Lost Creek," possibly more. The final trip, which carries the strongest support, in my mind, was in the early spring of 1901, when he and a companion named Bert Johnson crossed the divide and began prospecting the tributaries of the Salcha River. To his delight, Pedro found flood gold among the gravels of one of the streams. Thinking he had found his "Lost Creek," he named the creek 98 Creek. As the story goes, due to the spring runoff, the water was too high at that time to do any serious mining, so he and Johnson returned to Circle City to get more supplies and tell their friends of the discovery.

Jim: If I'm not mistaken a good size group assembled to accompany Pedro back, including Jack Kinnaly, along with Frank and Jack Costa. There was some confusion as to whether Tom Gilmore was or was not with the party. I would imagine that Bert Johnson was among the group. Were there more?

Terrence: Yes there were several others—a total of nine. These nine men were, up until that time, perhaps one of the most well-equipped groups of prospectors to ever go on a unified search in the Tanana Valley.

Jim: There were several presentations on this excursion. Many were contradictory and some within themselves were contradictory regarding the chronology of events. However, each of them carried some exciting events or details not held by others. I personally liked the continuity held in *Crooked Past*. During your research for that book, Terrence, did you encounter many of the same problems with clarity of time and people?

Terrence: Yes I did, Jim. We have to understand that most of this information was written well after the event. These men who first entered this unexplored country were like Pedro—they didn't have a clear idea of where they were all the time. Felix was the model of the rest. He didn't follow the crowd. He didn't stay in the Klondike for the easy riches and he didn't go to Nome. People with the same lust for adventure were fanning out at that time all across Alaska—the Kobuk, the Koyukuk, the Copper River and the Susitna River to name a few. These people, like Pedro, were dedicated to finding their own strike, and I think it goes along with what you said earlier: "Felix Pedro was a prospector not a miner." These men, like Pedro, loved the thrill of the search. The prize was the discovery. It is only natural for the events to become distorted with time. The events surrounding Pedro's many trips into the Tanana Valley become clouded; where he was, who he was with and the time he was there, fade with time, as do memories. When one considers this natural clouding of memories, it is clear that many times the stories may not be presented without distortion. While there were a couple of other directions I could have gone, I filtered out what was the most plausible for me in presenting the book *Crooked Past*. At 98 Creek the group of prospectors arrived, staked claims and immediately began to drop prospect shafts. Within a short period of time they had dropped eight to ten holes to bedrock, and while there were specks of gold dust within the gravels from top to bottom and a few flakes found at bedrock, the results were disappointing and the men became discouraged and blamed Pedro for leading them on a wild goose chase for a phantom rich gold-bearing creek. They had used up valuable time and much of their food for nothing. They nicknamed Pedro the "Old Witch," and split up into smaller prospecting groups, leaving Pedro alone on 98 Creek.

Jim: This is where there is some confusion regarding time and companions. Some researchers suggest that Gilmore was not with that party and Pedro returned to Circle City for more supplies, and that is where he teamed up with Gilmore. Others suggest that Gilmore was with the party and that he and Felix teamed up when they left 98 Creek. In addition, there are conflicting reports regarding exactly what year it was—1901 or 1902. Many events fall into position if the time is placed in the spring and early summer of 1901. Furthermore, if Gilmore was not with the party the companion issue becomes a little bit more understandable—Felix would have had to return to Circle City for supplies and to meet Gilmore. And there is one other issue that should be covered here. Felix Pedro, regardless of being nicknamed the "Old Witch," was regarded by many to be a careful and competent prospector. He had been followed many times by others to get the advantage of his superior knowledge of the creeks in the Tanana Valley. This trip with Gilmore was perhaps no exception.

Terrence: Yes, I think you're right on your conclusion. Wickersham, in his book *Old Yukon,* indicated that the prospectors often followed Felix. But also, there were a few more prospectors coming into the country at that time. For several years they had been prospecting and mining gold on the Birch Creek and Fortymile River side of the Yukon-Tanana Uplands and I believe that Pedro's thinking, as well as many other prospectors, was that if there is gold on one side of the Tanana hills there should be gold on the other. Some of the men who had accompanied Pedro to 98 Creek teamed up and continued to prospect in the Tanana Valley for the remainder of the summer, rather than return to Circle City. In addition, if I recall correctly, several parties traveling by boat up the Tanana had wintered over the past couple of years, and of course there was the Belt and Hendrick's Trading Post on the Tanana, at the mouth of the Chena. So yes, there were prospectors in the area, and many of them were interested in what Pedro and Gilmore were up to. The two men began prospecting along the Little Chena and ultimately ended up on Bear Creek. From Parker's research in 1929, a lot went on between Little Chena and Bear Creek.

Jim: Exactly. Those were some exciting events and any summary of Pedro's life wouldn't be complete without them. There is some ambiguity, but it seems that the two men made their way over the divide to the Little Chena River and up just past the mouth of Fish Creek, and that is where Felix Pedro panned their first colors. While the discovery of a few specks of fine gold was encouraging, it was not enough to indicate the presence of a valuable placer. They crossed over the divide into Quartz Creek, where they sank five prospecting shafts, but in each case they were flooded out and never reached bedrock. Discouraged, they went back across the divide to the mouth of Fish Creek with the intention of prospecting Fairbanks Creek, which later would yield a fortune in gold. However, at the mouth of Fairbanks Creek they came upon an encampment of un-friendly Indians who were uncomfortable with the white men prospect-ing in their hunting area. Where the story gets interesting is, just as Pedro and Gilmore were about to leave the Indian camp one of the In-dian children fell and ran a willow into his thigh, and at the sight of the blood the entire group of Indians frantically begged the white men to, "Fix 'm up." Pedro played the role of medicine man and washed the wound with soap, covered it with ointment and wrapped it with cloth. Following this act of kindness, the Indians told Pedro and Gilmore to go up the next creek and they would find "plenty much gold." While Pedro and Gilmore thought that Fairbanks Creek looked more promising, and would have preferred to prospect there, they didn't want to antagonize the Indians, and moved over to the next creek, where they set up camp and began digging prospect holes. They piled the gravel into dumps, which they later panned out. Meanwhile a bear wandered into camp and they shot it and captured its two small cubs and made pets out of them. From that time on the creek was named Bear Creek. Only one of the shafts was dug the full 22 feet to bedrock. However, all the gravels from all the prospect holes were panned, and yielded just $2.50. This is where, chronologically, events become a bit hazy. From a combination of all the literature and, as you say Terrence, presenting the most plausible story, it can be suggested that with what money and gold they had, plus the bear skin, the two prospectors left Bear Creek and headed down the valley to a point about a mile below the present site of Fox, where once again they panned colors from stream gravels. Here once again we have a divergence in the events. The presentation by Parker suggests that they followed Gold Stream to the foot of Ester Dome, where they encountered a party of four men. Interestingly, these four men with pack horses had followed Pedro and Gilmore, believing the partners were on the route to a find. Normally Pedro and Gilmore would not have welcomed company, but their supplies were running low and they needed help blazing their way through the brush and crossing bogs and streams. Six men working together could progress much more easily than two. They turned up Ester Dome thinking they could survey the area and establish a route. It was while on the dome that they sighted a boat—the *Lavelle Young*—maneuvering along the Chena River. As they continued to watch, the boat stopped and tied up at a heavily forested bend on the south side of the river. The prospectors were running severely low on supplies and recognized that it would be a heaven-sent opportunity if they could acquire some from the party on the boat. The way this version goes, it had been raining hard for the past couple of weeks and streams and bogs were full and all but impassable. It took Pedro and the others three days to build foundations for the horses to walk on and to cross flooded streams and gullies to reach Noyes Slough, just two miles from where the *Lavelle Young* was tied up on the south side of the Chena River. Now once again there are some uncertainties. It is suggested that Pedro and another man went forward on foot, but it was not clear whether that other man was Gilmore or not. Regardless, the men were successful in acquiring provisions and having them landed on the north side of the river. The other version and the one most commonly agreed on in the literature is the one presented in *Old Yukon* by Wickersham. Admittedly he was very thorough about the information he produced and I wouldn't be surprised if his wasn't the more accurate. It was the one that you used in your thesis, wasn't it Terrence?

Terrence: Yes, the version presented by Wickersham and presented in my thesis was much different than the one presented in the Parker-Gilmore interview. Then again, we have to remember that that interview was done in 1929, and the version by Wickersham, who by the way was also a personal friend of Felix Pedro, was done in 1903, just after the strike. Wickersham's version was first published in the *Fairbanks Miner,* which was his little newspaper. Then later he incorporated it into his book, *Old Yukon.* But we have a giant contradiction in these two sources; one suggests that Pedro was with Frank Costa, while the other said he was with Tom Gilmore. I chose to go with Gilmore because of the Parker interview. That's an example, Jim, of how a lot of this history is speculation. There is no way to check the information, especially in Fairbanks where, unlike the Klondike and Nome, where there were a lot of people keeping records, in Fairbanks there were very few—perhaps less than a half dozen or probably two or three. The most favorable account focused on 1901 when Pedro and Gilmore were sinking prospect holes on Bear Creek, which as you pointed out got its name when Felix shot a bear and made pets out of its cubs. They continued to prospect the Fish Creek valley through the remainder of the summer, fighting the bears and the mosquitoes. It seems that they spent a lot of time working in the mud and gravels for very little return, and they were almost out of food. Of course this meant that they would have to walk 165 miles back to Circle City to get more supplies. On August 6, 1901, they started the journey. They climbed their way up the wooded hill later named Pedro Dome. It was while the two men had stopped for a rest that they saw smoke rising in the distance. It could have been a forest fire or an Indian camp, but they looked through their field telescope and recognized it was the smoke from a steamboat. This they saw as an opportunity to resupply their outfit, winter over in the Tanana, and save themselves a 330-mile trip to Circle City and back. That is, if the people on the riverboat had supplies they were willing to sell. They continued to watch as the riverboat attempted unsuccessfully to get by the shallow Bates Rapids on the Tanana then return to the mouth of the Chena and attempt to navigate up the Chena. The two prospectors made their way down the dome and began the trek down the valley in hopes of flagging down the boat before it left. It took them at least a day, maybe two, to reach the Chena, where the boat was docked at a wooded area on the south side of the river. When they arrived, men were unloading freight in a clearing they had made in the woods. So you see, there is quite a variation in the two accounts of how Felix Pedro ultimately came into contact with the riverboat *Lavelle Young,* and what he and Gilmore went through to meet E.T. Barnette.

Jim: Can you give us a brief summary on who E.T. Barnette was and his history before beginning his trip into the Interior of Alaska to start his trading post?

Terrence: I would be happy to, Jim. In a nutshell, Eldridge Truman Barnette was 34 years old and living in Helena, Montana, when word of the fabulous gold strike in the Yukon of Canada was heard around the country in 1897. Several days later he was on a train heading for Seattle and the Klondike. Like many of the men living on the frontier he seemed to have no past, and like most of the others he wanted to keep it that way. Barnette arrived in Seattle on August 2, 1897, and although obtaining passage on any ship was all but impossible, he was able to book passage with the Northern American Trading and Transportation Company all the way to Dawson. This was called the "Rich Man's Route," because rather than the rigors of packing their gear across the Chilkoot or White Pass, the stampeders would take an ocean steamer to St. Michael—to the far west on the Bering Sea near the mouth of the Yukon River—then they would board a sternwheeler that would take them up the Yukon to Dawson. He, along with 160 other eager passengers, boarded the steamer *Cleveland*, a steamship with a rotten hull and an equally rotten reputation for being unlucky. The trip was a story in itself, but somehow, following several serious incidents and delays they made it to St. Michael only to learn to their horror that the sternwheeler that was to take them up the Yukon had left several hours earlier. While it may have sounded unlucky, for E.T. Barnette it was just the beginning of a long string of accidents that would help him become one of the most powerful men in Alaska. There was more bad news. The travelers were told frightening stories about the food shortage in Dawson and were advised to turn back. I remember one fellow who was a colorful storyteller and friend of E.T. Barnette's saying, "Some of the weaker-kneed Sisters, with shivers running down their spines, took advantage of the opportunity of returning on the *Cleveland*, while the more hardy figured that if they could come through such an experience as had been offered them on the *Cleveland* in safety, they would be safe in the hands of the Almighty pretty near anywhere." A few days later the little Jesuit mission steamer *St. Michael* steamed into St. Michael harbor. Sixty of the *Cleveland's* stranded passengers, the hardy souls who did not want to turn back, bought the vessel for $10,500, picked E.T. Barnette as their captain because he had some riverboating experience, loaded the *St. Michael* and a barge with their provisions, and began the trip up the Yukon to Dawson. Once again the trip was a story in itself, with many near disasters, but in each case the passengers were pleased with the efficiency with which Captain Barnette handled the situations. On September 28, 1897, when the little *St. Michael* landed in Circle City, ice had begun to form on the Yukon

River and the boiler on the boat was in very poor condition. Barnette resigned as captain, suggesting that it would be impossible to make the remainder of the trip to Dawson. Along with several others he off-loaded his gear. He would be stranded in Circle City for a couple of months, but he did have some money and he might have sold some of his provisions at a good profit because of the food shortage. He bought a dog team and, when the ground was frozen and would allow winter travel, he mushed on to Dawson. In Dawson he worked for awhile as manager of some mines for the North American Trading and Transportation Company. In the summer of 1898 he returned to Montana for a short period of time and married Isabelle Cleary before returning to the Yukon. During the next couple of years investments in trading supplies and mining claims evidently paid off. The return on his investment made Barnette more eager than before to set out on his own.

Jim: What was the story behind Barnette's interest in establishing a trading post at Tanana Crossing?

Terrence: In his travels Barnette had run into and become well acquainted with Jerome Healy. Healy had convinced Barnette that Tanana Crossing was going to be the gateway to the Interior of Alaska and anyone who had a trading post there would start the Interior's largest city. It was Healy's plans that caused Barnette to take on a couple of partners and go to Seattle in 1900 and purchase $20,000 in trade goods, which he intended to use to start his outpost at Tanana Crossing. He shipped the goods to St. Michael, located at the mouth of the Yukon River. In April of 1901 he traveled to Circle City and bought a steamboat called the *Arctic Boy* for $10,000, which he piloted down the Yukon to St. Michael, where he intended to load it with his trade goods and make the trip to Tanana Crossing. Barnette never did have good luck with steamers. One of his crew was taking the *Arctic Boy* for a trial cruise around St. Michael harbor when he hit a rock and tore the bottom out of the boat. There sat Barnette with 135 tons of supplies and no boat for shipping it.

Jim: This must be where Captain Charlie Adams enters the picture.

Terrence: That is exactly correct, and I suspect that Johne is probably a top authority on that particular bit of history.

Jim: Yes. Johne, I had the pleasure of attending the 2001 dedication of Felix Pedro's monument where you presented the birth of Fairbanks from a riverboat perspective. At that time you made mention of a personal acquaintanceship with Charlie Adams and his perspective on the trip with Barnette.

Johne: I really was honored to be asked and enjoyed giving that presentation. My information comes from an unbound and unpublished version of Charlie Adams' memoirs and Terrence's book. In addition, I feel very fortunate; I can remember direct stories from my father about working as pilot of the *Aksala* with Captain Charlie Adams, who had come out of retirement to help with the war effort during World War II. And that was the individual that actually piloted the boat that founded Fairbanks.

Jim: It's interesting that in just two generations it is possible to get a good portion of Alaskan history as far as being brought into modern civilization.

Johne: Yes, and it is exciting to sit here with this vantage point and know that 100 years ago the *Lavelle Young* steamed up the Yukon to the Tanana and finally unloaded Barnette and his freight on the shore of the Chena right down there.

Shann: Johne, how did Captain Adams and Barnette meet?

Johne: Well, E.T. Barnette was a riverboat captain and had a little stern-wheel steamer, as Terrence pointed out, called the *Arctic Boy*, which he intended to use to transport his 130 tons of trade goods to Tanana Crossing. As we already heard, during a trial cruise around the harbor at St. Michael the boat hit a rock and sunk. Charlie Adams was in St. Michael at the time and witnessed that particular mishap. Barnette could only salvage the hardware out of the *Arctic Boy*; the hull was unsalvageable. There he was with all these trade goods and no ship. That is when he approached Charlie Adams and Thomas Bruce, co-owners of the steamer *Lavelle Young,* with his proposition. Captain Charlie Adams presented the meeting in a couple of interesting ways. I think the one you gave in your book was the most interesting, Terrence.

Terrence: Well that information was gathered from several different sources. When Barnette told Adams where he wanted to go with all these supplies, he thought Barnette was crazy. "I was dumbfounded," Adams said, "Valdez-Eagle Crossing? Why man, that's nearly 400 miles up the Tanana above Fort Weare! How are you going to get there?" Barnette said that he thought the *Lavelle Young* could make it.

Johne: Well I guess Adams began to think about it. In his memoirs he stated: "None of us had ever been up the Tanana River, but I heard that Captain Patterson had been up there with a small launch bringing log rafts down for the United States Army at Fort Weare—this is now called Tanana. Captain Patterson was in St. Michael at the time and I went to see him." Do you recall the conversation, Terrence?

Terrence: Yes. In one of his reports, Adams indicates that Patterson said, "My God, man, you can't get beyond Chena without a lot of luck. That's only about halfway to the crossing! I'm glad you're trying it, instead of me."

Johne: Patterson suggested that if Adams was going to try it, there were two pilots that he could hire at Fort Weare. Adams then returned to Barnette and later in his memoirs stated: "I then told Captain Barnette that it was very doubtful if we could get beyond the Chena Slough, and after some talk we made up a contract whereby we agreed to take him to the slough for so much a ton and, if possible, to take him and his outfit of 130 tons to Tanana Crossing for an additional sum per ton. It was also agreed that if we got beyond Chena Slough and could get no farther that Barnette would get off with his goods wherever that happened to be."

Terrence: Indeed Adams was skeptical, but Barnette convinced him. To make the trip a little more appealing Barnette promised to pay Adams $6,000. As you indicated Johne, the heart of the agreement was that portion of the agreement regarding the Chena, "if he could get no farther Barnette would have to get off with his goods."

Johne: Barnette must have been extremely convincing, because despite the warnings from others worried that the *Lavelle Young* might not survive the trip, Adams reported: "So we took his goods aboard, and also Mrs. Barnette, Mr. Smith (who was some kind of a partner) and three men. In the outfit he also had a dog team and a horse. We left St. Michael about the eighth of August and had no trouble reaching Fort Weare near the mouth of the Tanana. There we got the two pilots. In going up the Tanana we had to cut our own wood for the boiler, stopping each evening when we saw some dry trees."

Terrence: It is important to emphasize that the upper Tanana River was unknown by riverboats the size of the *Lavelle Young* and that these people were entering a frontier that was for the most part a true wilderness with a complete lack of any help. They were definitely dependent on their own experience and capabilities for survival, not only for the boat but for themselves. They finally made it to the mouth of the Chena, directly below Bates Rapids. When they arrived in 1901, Nathan Hendricks and George Belt had a small trading post under construction across from the mouth of the Chena.

Johne: Adams speaks of the Bates Rapids: "We went on up six or eight miles and came to where the river was all scattered out in a lot of channels, none of which was deep enough for us. The *Lavelle Young* was not a light-draft steamer and we did not have steam steering gear or a steam capstan. Without this equipment, if the boat got stuck the crew would have to winch it free by hand." After trying all the channels at Bates Rapids it was clear that the *Lavelle Young* could make it no farther, and according to Adams, Barnette agreed with him. Adams went on to write: "Captain Barnette then told me that an Indian had told him that perhaps we could go up the Chena Slough and get out into the Tanana again above this bad place and go on up to the Crossing. This we decided to do. We went back and started up the slough."

Terrence: That was quite an interesting story in itself. About 14 or 15 miles above the mouth of the Chena (the Indians called it the "Rock River"), the *Lavelle Young* once again ran out of water. The deckhands tied the boat up on the riverbank about noon, and Adams called Barnette up to the pilothouse where the two of them argued for almost an hour. Neither could understand the pigheadedness of the other. Barnette asked Adams to at least take him back downstream and unload him at Belt and Hendrick's trading post. Adams said, "That's not in the Contract. You know darn well it's downstream and we'll get stuck a dozen times."

Johne: That's right. Adams figured he would get stuck a few times and wanted Barnette to pay extra for the time it took to get off the river bars. Barnette also realized that a loaded boat could get jammed tight on a river bar and become difficult to get off, so he refused to pay extra. Adams argued that according to the contract Barnette should get off at that spot. In his memoirs Adams states: "We were in the pilothouse alone, and after an hour or so of debate he (Barnette) said that he had noticed a nice high, heavily wooded bank about six miles below and asked me to take him there. I agreed to do so. On the way down we got stuck twice, but not bad." Adams went on to say, "This was August 26, 1901, about four o'clock."

Terrence: It took a few days for them to prepare the site and unload the boat and it was during one of these days that Felix Pedro and Tom Gilmore appeared from the wilderness.

Jim: What was Barnette's reaction when he saw the two prospectors?

Terrence: I think he was both surprised and pleased to see his first customers.

Shann: Wickersham, in his book *Old Yukon,* suggests that, "The merchant and the miner—the only representatives of their classes then in the splendid Tanana Valley passed a pleasant evening aboard the boat."

Terrence: Yes, Pedro informed Barnette that he had found good prospects on several creeks in the area, but he had not yet made a strike. Barnette then shared his sad story about his broken plan of going to Tanana Crossing, about 200 miles up the Tanana River.

Jim: Wickersham also wrote, "then and there it was agreed to establish a post on the bank where the steamer was tied up." But from what has been written Barnette still had intentions of going to Tanana Crossing.

Terrence: That's true, it was confusing, but Barnette was making the best out of a real bad situation. What he said was that he would operate a trading post from there until he could move on to Tanana Crossing. He optimistically christened the post "Chenoa City." I thought as I wrote the book that that was a pretty big name for a clearing in the woods with a few tents and one unfinished log cabin.

Jim: I understand that Barnette sold Pedro and Gilmore a complete winter's outfit. If that was the case it suggests that the two prospectors wintered over in the Tanana Valley. Also Felix Pedro and Tom Gilmore were the first customers to purchase goods in what was to become Fairbanks, Alaska.

Terrence: I never thought of that, but they were the first customers in Fairbanks. As soon as Pedro and Gilmore loaded their pack animals with their supplies they disappeared into the woods, and Barnette returned to the task of unloading the boat and getting his supplies under shelter. He was still not convinced that being stranded on the Chena Slough was such a good idea.

Johne: I think everyone recognized the situation as bleak. Captain Adams wrote: "It looked very bad for Captain Barnette to be put off there with no Indians or anyone else to trade with," and "Mrs. Barnette was crying when we left the next day, as it did not look good to her either." He also commented that, "Captain Barnette was quite angry with me because I would not take him to the mouth of the slough."

Terrence: Just before Adams departed, Barnette gave him a bundle of letters to mail, but he would not shake hands with the captain of the *Lavelle Young*.

Shann: How many people were left with Barnette at "Chenoa City?"

Terrence: Well it was quite an unusual mix. Besides E.T. Barnette and Isabel Barnette, there was Jujiro Wada, a Japanese cook; "Shorty" Robinson; another fellow by the name of "Soapy Smith the second;" Jim Eagle, a frontiersman from New Brunswick; Ben Atwater, who was once declared the strongest man in the United States; and a former deck hand from the *Lavelle Young,* Dan McCarty.

Jim: From the literature it is gathered that Barnette was bitter about being left stranded on the bank of a small river hundreds of miles from where he wanted to be, with no hope of moving for another year.

Terrence: I like to say that Fairbanks was a town founded at the wrong place, at the wrong time, by the wrong person, on the wrong side of the wrong river, but other than that, it is just perfect.

Shann: I wonder what could have been going through Barnette's mind at that moment.

Terrence: Well I think that he had already started to make plans. In the bundle of letters that he sent out with Adams to be mailed was one to his brother-in-law, Frank Cleary, back in Montana, instructing him to catch a steamer to Valdez. That winter he sent Dan McCarty to Valdez to meet Frank and bring him back to Chenoa City. It was Dan McCarty that blazed the first trail to Valdez in the middle of the winter, arriving in late February. With Mrs. Barnette's brother, McCarty began the 400-mile return trip, but it was not easy. The two men got caught in a blizzard and ran out of food four days from the cache. It took three weeks for McCarty to recover from the trip, but as soon as he was rested, he, along with Captain Barnette, Isabelle Barnette, Charles Smith, and a mail carrier and dog musher by the name of Jim Huntington, who had recently made it into Chenoa City, departed for Valdez. Barnette left his brother-in-law, Frank Cleary, in charge of the cache, with instructions not to give credit to anyone.

Jim: What was Barnette's plan at that time, Terrence?

Terrence: Well, Barnette took out a large load of furs that he had taken in trade from the Indians and would sell in Seattle. While he was in Valdez a reporter interviewed him and Barnette said that his plan was to go outside and get a shallow draft boat that would make its way through Bates Rapids, which he suggested "can easily be done." He said that one day the Tanana was going to be very rich and he was going to bring in a bigger load of supplies for the trading post he intended to start at Tanana Crossing.

Johne: He was successful in purchasing a shallowdraft, flat-bottomed boat, which he named *Isabelle* after his wife. The boat had been shipped in pieces and had to be assembled at St. Michael for the trip to the Interior of Alaska.

Terrence: Several months after they left Alaska they were back at St. Michael assembling the boat, when Barnette ran into Judge Wickersham. This is an important point regarding the naming of Fairbanks. One day while they were making preparations to leave, Judge Wickersham came by and Barnette and he sat down on a piece of driftwood. As they watched the workmen put the finishing touches on the boat, Barnette told Wickersham of his plans to start a new town at Tanana Crossing. It was at that time that Wickersham asked Barnette to name his new trading post "Fairbanks" after Senator Charles W. Fairbanks of Indiana, a man who was the force behind Judge Wickersham's judicial appointment to Alaska. Barnette saw the advantage of having someone in a position of power as an ally and agreed to the suggestion. The two men shook hands on the name "Fairbanks." There have been several other suggestions regarding how Fairbanks got its name, but Wickersham, in his book *Old Yukon,* is very clear where the name originated, and that was between him and E.T. Barnette as they stood on the beach at St. Michaels and shook hands in agreement.

Johne: I am not certain where I read this, perhaps it was in your book Terrence, but the way I understand it the *Isabelle* left St. Michael in August and arrived without any major incidents at the mouth of the Chena in early September.

Terrence: That is right, and the water was so low that he couldn't get the *Isabelle* up the Chena to his cache. At that time he thought that if he couldn't even get this shallow-draft boat as far as the *Lavelle Young* had made it the year before how would he ever get it past Bates Rapids and up the river to Tanana Crossing. Four miles below his cache the Isabelle stuck fast to a sandbar and they could go no farther—Barnette was trapped.

Jim: Meanwhile things had been happening in the Tanana Valley. Let me refresh your memories. Barnette left his brother-in-law, Frank Cleary, in charge of running the trading post in "Chenoa City." Just before he left, Barnette told Cleary, "Do not give any credit to anybody." Now this is the story that is pretty well accepted. During that winter of 1901—02 Felix Pedro and Tom Gilmore continued to look for the "Lost Creek." By April they were about out of supplies and showed up at Barnette's cache. The two men had only $100 between them—not enough for a full outfit—but 25-year-old Frank Cleary, even though he had been told by Barnette not to give credit, took the $100 and sold them a full outfit, charging the rest to his (Cleary's) personal account.

Terrence: Yes. And it is equally as well known that shortly after that, conditions began to go bad for Pedro for a short period of time. Tom Gilmore returned to Circle City, and Pedro was left alone to fight the mosquitoes and the bad weather as he dropped prospect shafts in the frozen ground along several creeks. Pedro had a bad heart, and in early July he once again appeared at Barnette's cache to get some more supplies and a stock of medicines.

Jim: This is a good point in the story to introduce the fact a little more strongly that Pedro, even though he had been dubbed the "Old Witch" a year earlier, was still recognized as a careful and competent prospector, and as a result he had been followed many times by others hoping to benefit from his superior information and knowledge of the creeks. At this particular time, without the security of his companion Tom Gilmore, he was even more uneasy about others spying on his activity. He often camped a long distance away from his actual prospect hole to keep from drawing the attention of others. That was exactly how it was when he discovered gold lacing the gravels of Pedro Creek. He camped on Fish Creek, and each day he would cross over the ridge. And when his rich prospects became a certainty he was even more worried that the camp followers would descend on the creek before he could locate claims for his friends. He continued to secretly prospect both Pedro and Cleary Creeks without building fires or engaging in any other activity that would attract attention. Finally, in a nervous condition, on July 22, 1902, he staked the best-known claims for himself and his friends. He had attempted to drop a prospect shaft to bedrock on Pedro Creek, but because of the weakened condition resulting from his bad heart, he was unable to complete the shaft. He did however recognize that there was considerable gold from the surface downward. Because of his poor health he decided to travel to the trading post. Does anyone recall the date that he returned to Barnette's cache?

Terrence: Yes, he showed up at Barnette's store on July 28. I think that Cleary might have been surprised to see him back so soon. Pedro was very excited and he took Cleary to the side and told him he had "Struck It." At last he had discovered gold in the Tanana Valley. Pedro said that he had been working about 12 miles to the north, with a shovel, on a small creek below a dome (later to be named Pedro Dome). He wasn't certain how rich the creek was, but this time he knew he had made a big discovery.

Jim: The way I understand it he made known his good luck to a few friends then at the trading post. Frank Costa, Cleary and a couple of other friends immediately stampeded off to stake more claims.

Terrence: I think at first Pedro was worried that there might be another stampede like the time he thought he had discovered the "Lost Creek," and I don't think he liked the title of "Old Witch," so he wanted to make certain the ground was as good as he thought, and secondly he wanted to make certain that if the ground was as good as it looked that his friends would have the best claims. In the month that followed, Pedro located four other discovery claims on four creeks surrounding Pedro Dome, including Cleary, Gold, Twin and Gilmore Creeks. He may never find "Lost Creek," but he was going to make certain that he didn't lose these.

Jim: This brings us to a discrepancy in time and different claims. Wickersham suggests that Cleary and McCarthy made their way over to Circle City to record the claims. During that same period of time a fellow by the name of Ed Quinn, along with another fellow by the name of Smallwood, began to help Pedro. To keep the camp followers from spotting them they worked at night completing the shaft to bedrock on Pedro Creek, and there found a large concentration of "glittering" gold. Along with Pedro's other friends that were at Barnette's cache and knew of the discovery, as you mentioned Terrence, he began to prospect and stake claims on other creeks in the area. Wickersham suggests that it was Cleary and Dan McCarty that made their way through the wilderness to Circle City to record the claims; however, from what Ed Quinn reported, it was he who went to Circle to record the claims. It is safe to conclude that because Cleary was in charge of the trading post he did not go, but rather it was Ed Quinn that first went to Circle to record the claims.

Shann: Didn't Pedro stake and record claims for a lot of his friends?

Jim: Yes, and that shows us just what kind of man Felix Pedro was. At the trading post he quietly informed his friends of the discovery, and out on the creeks he staked claims for all those who had helped him out during the earlier years. Some who were memorable included Joe Miller, known as "Portuguese Joe," who grubstaked Pedro for one of his trips, and who received No. 1 above Discovery; Tom Gilmore, his partner, received No. 2 below Discovery. None of his friends, including August Hanot the man who had so much faith in Felix, were forgotten; they were repaid by having rich claims staked in their names.

Shann: Where was Barnette during this time?

Terrence: Well, in early September as I said earlier, the *Isabelle* turned up the Chena River and Barnette found the water so low that he couldn't even make it to his cache. Finally, four miles below the cache, the *Isabelle* got stuck on a sandbar and Barnette and his crew were forced to hike the remainder of the way to the cache.

Jim: One account suggested that when Barnette arrived at the cache and learned that his brother-in-law, Frank Cleary, had given credit to Pedro, he was furious, stating something to the effect that, "a wandering prospector was not the most reliable credit risk." When Cleary quieted Barnette down he said, "Wait a minute. He has made the strike that's going to make this a gold rush town." Barnette, seemingly already despondent about the Tanana Crossing project, abandoned his plans and made the decision to stay right where he was; like you said Terrence, "in the wrong place, at the wrong time and on the wrong side of the wrong river, but other than that it was just perfect."

Terrence: That is true, and as soon as Barnette and his crew heard the full story they dropped what they were doing, grabbed some provisions, and left the boat and the cache in the hands of the cook and Mrs. Barnette, as they raced off to Pedro Creek.

Jim: It appears that this is where the two men's similar dispositions came together. They were both driven towards their particular goals. Pedro was driven to discover a new goldfield and Barnette was driven to establish a trading post that would be the center of trade in the Interior of Alaska. That was the day that both men's dreams came true; stampeders began to filter into the Tanana Valley and Chenoa City began to grow. The gold was not as easily recovered in the Tanana as in the Klondike or Nome, where it was found on the surface or at depths of 40 feet or less. The deposits in the Tanana were deeply buried, often to depths of 100 feet or more. In some cases it was as deep as 200 feet. Many of the stampeders who filed into the region became discouraged and left, stating that the deposits in the Tanana were worthless.

Shann: The deeply buried paystreaks were the reason that the goldfield was slow to develop. It didn't reach its peak until 1909. Before then it was necessary to transport in the steam equipment necessary to allow profitable mining of the deeper ground. At that time Cleary and Fairbanks Creeks were identified as the most valuable in the area. In all, by 1909 approximately $40 million in gold was extracted from the frozen ground.

Jim: When was the name of Chenoa City officially changed to Fairbanks?

Terrence: Well it didn't take long, and perhaps Barnette, thinking he was in the middle of another Klondike, was eager to get that name accepted. On September 10, ten days after he arrived back into the Tanana Valley, a miners meeting was held in Felix Pedro's tent on Pedro Creek. Barnette was selected as the local recorder, and it was at that meeting that Barnette convinced the miners to adopt the name of "Fairbanks" for the town he believed would build up around his trading post.

Johne: When did Wickersham arrive on the scene?

Terrence: Wickersham arrived in the spring of 1903. He thought the place looked like a pig sty. Wickersham described the view of Fairbanks from across the river as he first saw it as a few log structures accompanied by a few tents set in a clearing of a primeval forest. At that time there was a rivalry for supremacy with Beltz and Hendricks, who had established a trading post at the mouth of the Chena, where it entered the Tanana River, and which they simply called "Chena." A little later they courted Wickersham in an attempt to get the courthouse established in Chena, but Wickersham true to his word with Barnette to do anything he could to make his trading post successful if he named the new town Fairbanks established the courthouse at Barnette's trading post. This decision, along with its proximity to the goldfields, guaranteed the future of Fairbanks.

Jim: During that year, our central figure, Felix Pedro, was very busy working his claims. Before we move on, let me comment on the confusion regarding who actually went to Circle City to record claims. After reading several articles it appears that there were two trips made. As pointed out earlier the first trip to Circle City was made by Ed Quinn to record Pedro's claims, claims for himself and claims for other men on the creeks of the area with Commissioner Charles E. Claypoole. The second trip was made after more claims were staked by some of the men who stampeded in after learning of the strike from Ed Quinn. By compiling the results of several sources it seems that the second trip (reported by Wickersham) made by Dan McCarty and Frank Cleary occurred after Barnette returned and the miners had their meeting in Pedro's tent. At that meeting Barnette was selected as recorder and the name of the trading post was changed from Chenoa City to Fairbanks. The entire sequence was vague, and it was unclear why the men went to Circle City to record their claims after Barnette had been selected as recorder, but that is what appears to have occurred regarding the registration of claims. Regardless, the richness of the ground had been established and the future of Fairbanks was certain.

Shann: There were quite a number of stories regarding the value of the ground in the new gold camp. Perhaps one of the reasons is that the gold lay deeply buried in paystreaks. The paystreak was relatively shallow on Pedro Creek, compared to other creeks in the area. Pedro Creek was only about 20 feet to bedrock while, as pointed out before, gold in other creeks lay as deeply buried as 100 feet and in rarer cases 200 feet.

Jim: That is probably the reason so many stampeders thought the deposits in the Tanana Valley were worthless. It was impossible for solitary miners without steam equipment to drop prospect shafts through over 100 feet of frozen ground. It would take several weeks and in many cases there would be no gold to reward them for their expenditure of time and effort.

Shann: Following his arrival, Judge Wickersham wanted to check the value of the claims for himself. As a consequence, he took a trip out to the mines. The following report is based on his observations:

"The writer made a personal inspection of the mines on Gold Stream, Pedro and Cleary Creeks. A dozen pans from the top of the dump on Pedro's discovery claim on Cleary Creek yielded an average of over seven cents to the pan. Noble brought five pans from the face of the drift in the shaft and they yielded twenty-five cents to the pan. The pay streak is located for more than 100 feet in width and 800 feet long on this claim and is at least six feet thick. On No. 2 above on Pedro Creek Jack Costa's claim, the dump yielded eight cents to the pan, and Costa informed us that his pay streak had been located 150 feet wide, six feet deep and the length of his claim. A rough calculation shows that if his statement is correct there is about half a million dollars in his claim. Discovery on Pedro panned as well as Costa's. On Gold Stream Dan McCarty's claim panned an average if eight cents and Willig's but little less.

Pay has been located for six miles or more on Pedro and Gold Stream into which Pedro empties. Cleary Creek heads just over the low divide from Pedro and extends the placer ground that much farther north. Coarse shot gold has been located on Fairbanks Creek, and prospecting is being pushed on a number of other tributaries of Gold Stream and Fish Creek. Rich pay is known to exist on at least three creeks—Pedro, Cleary and Gold Stream, and the future of the camp is beyond doubt. Other creeks are prospecting high and the prospectors are confident. What the creeks need is systematic and careful prospecting."

Johne: It was never clear if Fairbanks was a colorful gold rush camp similar to Dawson and Nome. It always seemed that unlike the other two camps, which exploded into history because of the discovery then slowly declined, Fairbanks was just the opposite.

Jim: Exactly, and that was because the gold on the majority of the creeks was so deeply buried. As you indicated, Johne, the deposits in the Tanana Valley were slow to develop and, as Shann pointed out, this was because it took some time to bring in the equipment suitable to mine the deep ground. The Fairbanks Mining District didn't reach its peak until 1909. A lot happened to Felix Pedro in those years and the years that followed.

Shann: A year following the discovery Fairbanks was still very much a frontier village consisting of a few log buildings and tent structures, each accompanied by the customary outhouse. All this was in a setting of a few trees and many stumps—remnants of the trees from which the log buildings were constructed. It was in this setting on April 28, 1903, that one of the most interesting social events was reported by Wickersham in his newspaper, the *Fairbanks Miner,* and later in his book *Old Yukon* and that was the "Bar Banquet."

> "The first banquet in the Tanana country was given one night in true frontier style in the Tokio Restaurant on Second Avenue. The Tokio in outward appearance lacked Japanese architectural style, for it was a ten by twelve Seattle tent with a redhot Yukon stove in a lean-to at the rear, for its cookery. Seven lawyers who had come in off the trails were all bidden to attend, and as prospective clients had to be invited to gladden the occasion, half a dozen $500-millionaires, made suddenly rich by the recent location of wildcat mining claims, were also requested to be present. The table of whipsawed spruce boards was covered with a dainty napery of flour sacks, beautifully ornamented in large letters carrying the name of the mill and the weight and brand of the contents; nail kegs served as dining-room chairs, and the viands and liquors were the best the country could produce."

"The menu was done by the official scrivener in his best letter press on birch bark. The menu was particularly interesting."

"Hiyu-Muck-a-Muck.

Hootch—Chena Cocktails, (a stout brew prepared by Hootch Albert a local boot legger).

Consommé, a la Tawtilla. (Heaven knows what that was)

Olives.

Chicken Mayonaise, Oyster paties.

Sauterne.

Wine Jelly, Cream Sauce.

Roast Moose, Prospector Style.

Mashed Potatoes, Green Peas.

Ice Cream—Yuma Canned.

Jelly Cake.

Nuts, Raisins, Cheese, Coffee,

Cigars."

"The wine list included Hootch Albert's Best Brew, served in tin cups (no glasses in camp). Pedro's gold pan was used as a tray." Following the feast there were speeches and toasts to a late hour. "Pedro presented his battered, long carried discovery gold pan, and the first ounce of gold-dust off his first Tanana claim to be forwarded as a present from Tanana miners to the Camps god-father, Senator Fairbanks of Indiana. What we lacked in style at that historic banquet we made up in good cheer."

Jim: Now that you mention it, I remember that story. It also confirms what you have said, Terrence. Fairbanks was named after Senator Fairbanks of Indiana. Since we are telling stories let me share one that stands out as the most recognized words ever spoken in the Fairbanks Mining District. It happened when Judge Wickersham first arrived in the country. Jack Costa, an Italian immigrant referred to commonly as "Happy Jack," who had claim No. 2 above Discovery on Pedro Creek, was just climbing out of his prospect hole with a pan of rich gravel in his hand when Wickersham arrived and the first words Wickersham ever heard issue from "Happy Jack" Costa's lips was, **"Oh by Godda, I gotta de gold!"**

Shann: It was words like those that echoed around the country. Men began to stream into the Tanana Valley by the thousands over the next few years. Gold production in that first year was meager at about $40,000, but by 1905 production had increased to $6,000,000 and the town of Fairbanks had grown to several thousand.

Jim: Throughout the next couple of years, like the other miners, Pedro began to prosper as he continued to mine and prospect in the Tanana Valley, staking more claims and of course setting up mining operations on his claims. His holdings included discovery claims and interests in discovery claims on Pedro Creek, Gilmore Creek, Goldstream Creek, Fox Gulch, Fish Creek, Bear Creek, Kokomo Creek, Fairbanks Creek and Twin Creek. Two men who played a big role in Felix Pedro's life arrived to work with him. These were his longtime friend and benefactor, August Hanot, and his son August Hanot Jr. In 1905 Felix decided it was time to find a wife and settle down. Massimo you probably know more about Felix's search for a bride. Why don't you fill us in.

Massimo: Well, as you said, Jim, Felix began his search for a bride. He told friends that while the American women were fine, he felt that the most desirable women were to be found at his birthplace in Fanano, Italy. He still had visions of the raven-haired beauty that he left behind when he hurriedly left the country. He left Fairbanks on a boat in the early summer of 1905 and planned to return to Fairbanks the next spring with his bride. While he was away August Hanot and August Hanot Jr. looked after his claims on Pedro Creek, and a fellow by the name of Ed Jones took care of his claims on Fairbanks Creek. When he arrived in Trignano and told the story of his success in the goldfields of Alaska no one believed him. But they still remembered the gunshot. He continued his search for a bride. He began courting a dark-eyed schoolteacher. At first she says yes then a little later says no. Then still later she says yes again, but finally the answer is no, and Felix returns to Alaska alone. Felix's mind is made up and he is determined to find a wife. The gold alone did not completely satisfy him. He continued his search in Alaska, but at that time in Alaska there were very few women. He searched and finally had to settle on someone who wanted him for whatever reason, probably not love, rather than someone he wanted. DeArmond reported that on November 22, 1906, Felix Pedro married Irish-born Mary Ellen Doran, a longtime Fairbanks resident. He further suggested that the two newlyweds immediately left on a trip back to his old home in Italy and a tour of Europe. They returned to Fairbanks over the winter trail from Valdez in March 1907. It wasn't long after their return that old-timers recognized that the Pedros "didn't get along." Stanton Patty suggests that no one was surprised. Mary Pedro was a severe looking woman and although she worked hard, she was very serious about being known as "a proper person." This was quite a contrast to Felix, who was somewhat casual regarding his role in the discovery of gold and corresponding wealth. He enjoyed relaxed sociable activities such as telling and listening to stories with his longtime prospecting and mining friends. A quote directly from Patty: "In January, 1908, *The Nome Gold Digger* reported a newspaper story from Tacoma that Mrs. Pedro was seeking a divorce and alimony. She then was residing in Tacoma. Apparently, the divorce never occurred."

Jim: It was interesting that DeArmond reported that the Pedros left on a tour of Europe immediately following their marriage. I also believed this to be true until the work of Mullen, the Pedro family genealogist, brought Court Document 26221, Superior Court of the State of Washington, November, 1908, to Shann's and my attention. That particular document contains Felix Pedro's own words covering the events that surrounded the marriage. It also confirms much of what we have covered regarding his life to this point. I think it is appropriate to present the document's contents here for those who are not familiar with it.

Shann: Jim and I obtained a copy of the court document, which has the full presentation of both sides. It may be of value to provide a summary for clarity of chronology and intentions of both Mary and Felix Pedro.

Terrence: The Pedros, marriage has always been a cloudy issue that needed clarification. I for one would be genuinely interested in hearing the facts as they exist in that document.

Shann: It contains several major components. These include, in chronological order:

1) Mary Pedro's complaint, Nov. 14, 1907

2) Mary Pedro's affidavit of serving summons, Nov. 14, 1907

3) Mary's settlement conditions, Nov. 14, 1907

4) Judge W.O. Chapman's order to serve summons on Felix Pedro, November 16, 1907

5) Summons to appear (unserved, Sheriff Thomas N. Morris), November 16, 1907

6) Mary Pedro's request for $1000 to be paid by Felix Pedro for depositions, January 27, 1908

7) Mary Pedro's affidavit of property settlement, January 27, 1908

8) Plaintiff's motion for temporary alimony and suit money, January 27, 1908

9) Memorandum of journal entry, January 25, 1908

10) Demurrer (no legal framework for complaint. Submitted by Felix Pedro's attorney), undated

11) Felix Pedro's response, March 24, 1908

12) Judge M.L. Clifford's order of attachment of Felix Pedro's Washington property, November 16, 1908

13) Attachment of Felix Pedro's Pierce County, Washington, property, November 16, 1908

14) Answer and cross complaint from Felix Pedro, May 20, 1908

15) Motion to strike, June 24, 1908

16) Order discharging writ of attachment, December 28, 1911

Copies are here for everyone.

Jim: As you can see, the romance certainly didn't last very long. They were married on November 22, 1906. Less than a year later, November 14, 1907, Mary Pedro filed for divorce in the Superior Court of the State of Washington for Pierce County. This raises a good many questions during a period of history when marriage and marriage vows, especially Catholic marriage vows, were held sacred. You studied this document closely, Shann. What was Mary's side of the story?

Shann: Well, the rumor from sources that you have already mentioned, Jim, was that Mary married Felix for his money and the divorce was simply a way for her to detach herself from the relationship with enough money to be comfortable for the rest of her life. Whether or not that is true I will leave to others to determine. The following is from the file that was begun by Mary Pedro on November 14, 1907: Mary Ellen Pedro, Plaintiff vs. Felix Pedro, Defendant:

"Comes now the above named plaintiff, and complains of the defendant, and for cause of action alleges:

I

That plaintiff was married to the defendant on the 22nd day of November, 1906; that there is no issue of said marriage.

II

That plaintiff and defendant continued to live together from the date of their marriage until the 1st day of August, 1907, on which date, without cause or provocation, defendant deserted and abandoned plaintiff, and left their home at Fairbanks, Alaska, without notice or knowledge or consent of the plaintiff, and his whereabouts ever since said date has been and still is unknown to plaintiff; that since said date, to-wit: August 1st, 1907, the defendant has wholly deserted and abandoned her; that plaintiff has no property or income or means of support, and is wholly dependent upon said defendant; that said defendant is a strong, able-bodied man, possessing large means amounting to Sixty-five Thousand Dollars, besides valuable property in Alaska; that notwithstanding, however, said defendant has refused and still does refuse to make suitable or any provision for said plaintiff, and has left plaintiff in a destitute condition.

III

That plaintiff is and for some time past has been an actual and bona fide resident of the State of Washington; and that defendant is well able to support the plaintiff.

IV

That the amount necessary for the support of the plaintiff is three thousand dollars per annum, payable monthly.

V

That the sum of two hundred and fifty dollars is a reasonable sum to be allowed plaintiff to be paid by the defendant as attorneys' fees for prosecuting this suit.

VI

That the defendant is the owner of the following described real estate situated in Pierce County, Washington:

The south half of the northeast quarter of the southeast quarter of the southeast quarter of section nine (9), township twenty (20) north, range four (4) east, of the value of fifteen hundred dollars; that said defendant is also the owner of a note signed by one William Scheers, dated March 18, 1902, payable to Herman Brending; that to secure the payment of said note said Scheers gave to said Brending a mortgage on the south half of the northwest quarter of the southwest quarter, and the north half of the southwest quarter of section ten (10), township twenty (20) north, range four (4) east; That said note was given for the sum of three thousand dollars; That thereafter the said note and mortgage were assigned to said Felix Pedro, and that said assignment is now of record in volume 140 of Mortgages, page 160, records of the Auditor's office of Pierce County, Washington.

VII

That the said defendant has disposed of his property to defraud the plaintiff herein, and for the purpose of placing his property beyond the reach of the court, and for the purpose that the defendant is about to dispose of his property with intent to defraud his creditors and especially with intent to defraud this plaintiff, and to avoid the payment of moneys necessary for her support and maintenance.

Wherefore, plaintiff prays judgment that the said defendant be ordered and required to pay to the plaintiff out of the property and income of the defendant the sum of three thousand dollars per annum, payable monthly, as well as the sum of two hundred and fifty dollars attorney's fees, and for such other further and reasonable sum as the court shall deem proper to be paid to her as and for her separate maintenance; plaintiff further prays that all sums awarded her may be declared to be a lien upon the property real and personal, hereinabove described, and that she may have execution issued upon said property and the sale thereof in default of any payment required by decree; and for the costs and disbursements of this action, and for such other and further relief as to the court may seem just and equitable."

Jim: Seemingly, Mary was suing for separate maintenance, rather than divorce, by reason of the abandonment and desertion by Felix and his refusal to support her.

Shann: That is the way I understand it, but she continued her pursuit of his money. On the same day as Mary's complaint, her attorneys, Farrell, Kane and Stratton prepared a summons requiring Felix to appear within 20 days after service. Sheriff Thomas N. Morris was unable to locate Felix in Pierce County and the summons was unservable in Washington. In an affidavit prepared once again on November 14, 1907, Mary recognized that Felix was not in Pierce County and the summons would not be successfully served. As a result, she sent the summons to Fairbanks where she believed Felix resided.

Jim: In summary of the legal documents, it appears that November 14, 1907, was the day that Mary Pedro made her legal move to obtain life-long support from Felix. What makes all this so valuable is that it is fact; not what Mary says, but that what she says is documented. Never before was there so much as a letter found telling of Felix's life. While I focused on Felix, you have covered Mary's position regarding the marriage. It is unfortunate that she didn't provide more details regarding her experiences in the marriage. Seemingly she has only provided unsupported accusations to this point. It is interesting that they only lived together nine months and yet Mary felt she was entitled to what seems like such a large settlement, especially when one considers that in those days men were working for less than a dollar an hour.

Shann: But there is more. That same day Mary Ellen Pedro submitted an "Affidavit for Attachment." The following excerpt describes her intent:

> "that said defendant is a non-resident of the State of Washington; that said defendant conceals himself so that the ordinary process of law cannot be served upon him; that the defendant has removed and is about to remove his property from this state with intent to delay and defraud his creditors; that the defendant has signed, secreted and disposed of, and is about to assign, secrete and dispose of his property with intent to delay and defraud his creditors; that the defendant is about to convert his property into money for the purpose of placing it beyond the reach of his creditors; that said defendant has already converted a part of his property into money for the purpose of placing it beyond the reach of his creditors; that the defendant is about to dispose of his property with intent to defraud his creditors, and especially this plaintiff;

that the defendant has disposed of a part of his property with intent to defraud his creditors, and especially this plaintiff.

Wherefore, affiant asks for a writ of attachment to be issued in the above entitled action in the manner provided by law. Real estate only to be attached."

The affidavit was signed by Mary Ellen Pedro, November 14, 1907.

Jim: Again there seem to be a lot of accusations but no supporting documentation. What is clear is that she submitted all her affidavits and complaints on the same date.

Shann: Yes, and two days later, November 16, 1907, Judge W.O. Chapman ordered the sheriff's department to serve the summons. On that same day Deputy Sheriff Dolan reported:

"I made due and diligent search for, and was unable to find, said defendant in Pierce County, Washington, and I further certify upon information and belief that said defendant is a non-resident."

Jim: It seems strange that Mary sent Felix the summons in Fairbanks, Alaska, on November 14, 1907, and Judge Chapman didn't order it served until the 16th. I suspect there is more to this maneuvering.

Shann: On her behalf her attorney, James H. Kane expanded her request for money on January 27, 1908, by requesting an additional $1000 for witness depositions and to prepare her case for trial. On that same day, Mary presented an additional "AFFIDAVIT OF PLAINTIFF." It reiterated all that has already been said and added:

"that she is over the age of twenty-one years, and makes this affidavit on her own behalf as plaintiff for the purpose of obtaining funds for living expenses during the pendency of this action; that she has fully and fairly stated the case to her attorneys, Farrell, Kane & Stratton, and is informed and verily believes that she has a good and meritorious cause of action against the defendant herein; that she is unfitted for work, and is unable to support herself by her own exertions by reason of her present condition of health; that she has no money with which to pay for her living expenses..."

That was the extent of it, other than an unreadable memorandum of journal entry by Judge Clifford that was the summary of affidavits and complaints by Mary Pedro. You spent more time studying Felix Pedro's response, Jim. How did he reply and what was the outcome?

Jim: I don't know if the rest of you will agree, but in a way Mary Pedro did history a favor when she filed for separate maintenance. For the first time we have Felix's own words regarding his entry into the country and his life in Alaska. The first response was through his attorneys who presented the following "DEMURRER:"

> "Comes now the defendant, by his attorneys Williamson & Williamson and Burkey, O'Brien & Burkey, and demurs to the complaint on file herein for the following reasons: First. That the court has no jurisdiction of the person of the defendant or of the subject matter of the action. Second. That the plaintiff has no legal capacity to sue. Third. That the complaint does not state facts sufficient to constitute a cause of action."

Apparently this was not sufficient because Felix presented his response on March 24, 1908. His "Affidavit" presents a summary of his life in the United States and Alaska in addition to a much different and much more detailed story of his life with Mary Pedro following their marriage:

> "Felix Pedro, being first duly sworn on oath, deposes and says; that I am the defendant in the above entitled action; that I was born in Italy and am of the age of 49 years; that I came to the State of New York in the year 1881 and later moved to the State of Illinois, a short time thereafter and in the year 1884 came to the State of Washington, and went to work as a coal miner in the Town of Renton, near Seattle, Washington, and worked in that capacity for about two years, and then removed to Black Diamond, Washington, and engaged in the same line of work, and later on removed to Roslyn and from there to Carbonado and was engaged in these different places as a coal miner until some time in the year 1893, when I went to Cariboo, British Columbia, on a prospecting tour and was absent for about four months, returning to Kangley and residing there for a short time on a ranch I owned

at that place; affiant further states that in the year 1895 I went to Alaska and stopped at Forty Mile on the Yukon River and commenced mining and prospecting and continued so to do off and on until the year 1899; that about this time I came down to Circle City and went out prospecting and continued so doing until 1902 when I made a strike on what is known as Pedro Creek; where I have since said time continued to mine; that in the year 1905, in Gold Stream in the Fairbanks Mining District I met the plaintiff herein and in the fall of the same year I left Alaska and came out to the states and took a trip to the old country and returned to Fairbanks in the spring of 1906; that later in the year 1906, I left Fairbanks, Alaska and returned to the states and went to my ranch at Edgewood, Washington; that in the same year the plaintiff herein came to Seattle, Washington, and on the 22nd day of November, 1906, we were married at Tacoma, Washington, by the Rev. Father Hylebos of St. Leo's Roman Catholic Church, we being each members of that faith; affiant further states that in the spring of 1906 after the plaintiff and defendant had become engaged to be married, I bought the ranch at Edgewood, Washington, for the purpose of making a home for myself and wife, as the accommodations for home life were not very attractive in the northern country where my mines were located; that after our marriage on November 22nd, we went to Seattle, Washington, where we stayed a short time and then left for Hot Springs Arkansas, where we remained about six weeks, and we later left hot Springs about the middle of January and making a short stay at Kansas City and one or two other places we finally arrived in Los Angeles, California; that from the time of our marriage until our arrival in Los Angeles, the plaintiff seemed entirely dissatisfied with everything that I would do for her; if we went to one hotel to stop, she would object and want to go to another one claiming it was a little better than the previous place; she was constantly finding new ways to spend money and while I indulged every reasonable wish and demand she never was satisfied and was constantly dissatisfied and unreasonable; that after we arrived in Los Angeles she demanded that I pay her One thousand dollars ($1000), and I stated to her that I did not have that much money with me and was unable to do so; that I had paid her from the time of our marriage until our arrival in Los Angeles sums of money in excess of Five hundred and thirty dollars ($530) besides paying all our bills, and after my refusal to give her this One thousand dollars ($1000) she immediately left Los Angeles and started for Seattle, leaving all her baggage and trunks at the hotel and taking with her only two small hand grips. I had previously given her about all of the money I had with me and I could not leave Los Angeles until some few days later when I managed to meet a friend of mine from Alaska in Los Angeles who took me to the bank and arranged for my getting sufficient funds to follow on to Seattle; that upon my arrival in Seattle I commenced looking for the plaintiff and finally located her and used every endeavor possible to affect a reconciliation and could only do so upon the payment to her of the sum of one thousand dollars ($1000) demanded in Los Angeles, and knowing that we were husband and wife and that it was my duty to make every effort to get along with the plaintiff I paid her the one thousand dollars ($1000) hoping that sooner or later she would recognize that it was her duty as well as mine to make every reasonable effort to get along in peace and harmony, as the faith to which we both belong does not recognize a divorce, nor do I believe there is any occasion for the living apart of the plaintiff and myself, if the plaintiff will make any effort whatever to live with me in peace and harmony; that I requested the plaintiff to arrange our home on the ranch at Edgewood so that she might remain there while I returned to Alaska, I having purchased that ranch so that we might make our home there, and the plaintiff refused to remain on the ranch during my absence, I also offered the plaintiff to pay her board and lodging and expenses in Seattle, but she refused to remain in Seattle and I informed her that owing to the conditions in Alaska it would be manifestly impossible to provide her with any suitable home and that it would be much nicer and more suitable for her to remain there on the ranch or in Seattle until my return from Alaska which would only be a matter of a few months; but she refused to do so; that I spent on our trip from Seattle to Los Angeles, being gone about two months, a little over Fourteen hundred dollars ($1400), and after giving her the One thousand dollars ($1000) in Seattle on my return from Los Angeles I gave her in addition the sum of Two hundred dollars ($200) to have her teeth fixed and Two hundred dollars ($200) she claimed she wanted to loan a Mrs. Murray; affiant further states that he finally consented to take the plaintiff to Alaska with him, she fully understanding the conditions which awaited them in Alaska, and we left Seattle the later part of February or first of March, 1907; the party was composed of Miss O'Leary, Mrs. Pedro and myself. We got to Valdez and we stopped there, I think, two nights and from there we started on the road. We went down on the trail until we got to McDevitt's Road House. We were there for five or six days. The weather was very stormy. Then I was ready to go, and a party was going with the horses and empty sleighs going in for the Cold Storage Company, and I came back and asked her if she was going and she says, "Yes". Then I got the robe from the house over to the sleighs and came back and I said we were ready and she said she was not going. She says, "You can go yourself". My horse had become disabled on the road and died between McDevitt and Sullivan. I went on with the cold storage horses and she caught up to me, I think, at Sullivan, going by stage. There was no room for me on the stage and she told me she would meet me at the Golden Gate at Fairbanks. I followed on with another party and met her at the Golden Gate in Fairbanks. We stopped together at the Golden Gate for a few days, then I left to go out on the mining claims so as to arrange for a cabin for our home and I ordered some lumber and then I went down to Fairbanks and I met her on Fairbank Creek and then came over on foot to Pedro Creek and she came over on the stage and then she went to Fairbank Town and I started to go down to Fairbanks but I had to go back to see about this lumber to build the floor of the cabin. It not having arrived I went back to town and I asked her if she was coming over on the creeks and she says, "No, I am not going." She says, "I am not going until you have a cabin suitable for me to move into," and I told her she could come to the road house and stop there until I had it fixed up, and she said she would not stop to no road house. Then I went back to the creek and I stayed about a week and during this time the lumber for this cabin was used for something else and I took lumber from Discovery and fixed up a cabin suitable for her to live in and I came over and asked if she was coming and she says, "No, I am not going", and I told her I had no money and asked her if she had received the money she loaned Mrs. Murray, and she says, "No." I said I wished she would get it as I needed it, and she says, "You go get it." So I went back to the creek for some time, she all this time living in town. We continued to live in this manner, she in Fairbanks and me on the creeks, until the first of June, she all this time refusing to come out on the creeks and live with me in the cabin I had arranged for our home. In June she came out and she stayed there at the road house one night or two nights, then left and went visiting on some of the other creeks. She was there for about a week or so and then she returned to the road house at Pedro Creek where I was getting my meals and stayed there only two nights and then she went to Fairbanks and left me to fix up a cabin, she agreeing to come back on the creek and live with me, and went to Fairbanks to get provisions and other things to fix up the cabin for living purposes. Then she was in town about two weeks during this time I put a floor in the cabin, but it was not completed when she returned because I thought it would not be suitable for her and there was another cabin nearby, which I desired to show her to see if she would like it better than the one I was fixing up. It was now nearly the first of July when she came back. Then the cabin was suitable for her and she stayed there a month. She fixed up the cabin. She left about the last week in July to go to Fairbanks and promised to return with Miss O'Leary. Miss O'Leary returned to the creeks the early part of August without Mrs. Pedro. During all the time she was in Alaska she paid not attention to me whatever, seemed to have no use for me and did her best to humiliate me both privately and in public. She used intoxicating liquors to excess and my remonstances were of no avail, I did everything in my power to make her happy and to furnish her with as good a home as was possible in Alaska. Her conduct was the source of constant worry to me and she had me completely unnerved and when she failed to return as she had promised and I could get no word of where she was or what she was doing and knowing that I was failing both physically and mentally and that a continuance of her conduct was such that if I did not get away I would soon be unable to attend to my own business or know what I was doing. On about the 8th day of August I left Alaska for my ranch at Edgewood for a rest that I might recuperate my health and be in a position to know what was best to do to straighten out our difficulties. After my arrival at Edgewood I stayed about a month and then went east and later returned and most of the time since leaving Alaska until about two months ago my mental condition owing to her conduct has been such that it all seems a blank to me. About two months ago I underwent an operation performed by Dr. Wheeler of Tacoma, Washington and since my recovery therefrom my condition both mental and physical has been almost entirely recovered. Since my recovery of my health I have made every endeavor to so shape my affairs that I may be able to affect a reconciliation with my wife, and about three weeks ago I went to Seattle, Washington, where she is at present residing, and called on her in her rooms and told her that I wished she would return with me to our ranch at Edgewood and that I would do everything in my power to make life pleasant. I told her I was willing to make the home at Edgewood comfortable and to fix things as she desired, but she refused to come and live with me. That I have cash on hand of about three thousand dollars and I own the ranch a Edgewood of a probable value of Three Thousand dollars and I have an interest in certain mining claims in

Alaska, the value of which is problematical; that I received as my share from said mines last year the sum of Eighty-two hundred dollars and the parties who were running the mines for me claim that I owe them certain moneys for wages and supplies which they estimated to be five thousand dollars. That since having this trouble with my wife the parties who are running my mines and interested with me in them are causing me a great deal of trouble and have returned to Fairbanks and have threatened to commence litigation there against me and I am unable to go to Fairbanks and protect my interests there owing to this lawsuit with my wife. That the value of these said claims, even if they were not in litigation, is unknown and absolutely problematical, and it will take a great deal of money to be used for the working of these mines the coming summer; that I have had to send a representative to Fairbanks and pay his expenses to look after my interests upon said claims and the money I have on hand will not even be sufficient for the necessities and expenses of operating these mines the coming season. Affiant further says that there is no reason for the plaintiff and defendant living separate and apart; that he has a good home for her at Edgewood, Washington where she is welcome to come and stay and he believes that with her assistance he will be able to make her a comfortable and happy home and will be able to protect his interests in Alaska and with their joint efforts may be able to produce something from these mines so that they may be able to live properly for the balance of their lives. Affiant further says that the present litigation brought against him by his wife and the threatened litigation by his managers in Alaska were causing him a great deal of worry, and he believes that if the plaintiff herein could be freed from the domination of the parties who are inciting her against the defendant and if she would be left free to come and live at her home, which is her proper place, she would do so, but that if this court shall make an order for this defendant to pay her a separate maintenance she will refuse to return and live with him as it is her duty so to do; that both the plaintiff and defendant in this action are members of the Catholic church and divorce is not countenanced in that church and neither the plaintiff or defendant herein can marry again during the life of the other, and the defendant herein is desirous of having a home, that being what he has worked hard for the past twenty years, and he is now in a position to enjoy one and has located his home at Edgewood, Washington, which fact was well known by the plaintiff before her marriage to the defendant and the defendant herein will make every effort to make the home pleasant for the plaintiff and is willing and anxious that she should return to him and live there with him.

Affiant further says that he has no other assets except as herein set forth, all of which is needed for the protection of his property interests and the living expenses of himself and his wife at their home at Edgewood.

And further affiant saith not."

This document was signed "Felix Pedro" on the 24th day of March, 1908, and notarized by James F. O'Brien, Notary Public in and for the State of Washington, residing at Tacoma.

Shann: It seems like Mary wanted separate maintenance but not a divorce and that Felix wanted to remain married and in cohabitation.

Jim: Yes, up to the time of his deposition that was the way I understood it, Shann, however, when he presented his Answer and Cross Complaint On May 20, 1908, it was submitted just about the same until section V.

V

"That the defendant is a man of a nervous temperament and not strong physically and needs all the property which he now owns and which has been accumulated by his own toil for his future support and maintenance."

He began to recognize certain unfavorable aspects of his marriage which were seemingly out of his control. To correct these he concluded in section VI.

VI

"That the plaintiff never has had any affection for the

defendant, and has never shown any interest in him, and has been interested chiefly in the one pursuit of separating the defendant from his money and this defendant believes that the plaintiff is mainly interested in acquiring from the defendant as much of his property as she can, and has at all times had no further interest in him or his welfare."

From his previous affidavit we have become aware that Felix wanted to live with his wife in harmony on his ranch at Edgewood, Washington. He brings this to the Court's attention in Section VII of his Answer and Cross Complaint.

VII

"That the defendant has on different occasions offered plaintiff a home and has offered to live with plaintiff if she would do her part towards making their home a pleasant and a happy one, but the plaintiff has at all times refused to live with the defended, and has always insisted on a separate maintenance, which the defendant alleges is unjust and unnecessary."

Throughout his testimony Felix demonstrates Mary's intent on separating him from his money. He summarizes this in Section VIII of his Answer and Cross Complaint.

VIII

"That the plaintiff is a woman of mature years and has always earned her own living, and during the short time which she lived with defendant she had her living, which was paid for by this defendant, and has received from this defendant in addition thereto, sums aggregating about two thousand ($2,000), all this covering a space of about eight months."

Apparently Felix recognizes the futility of the marriage by this time and changes his attitude regarding the sanctity of matrimonial bonds as dictated by their common Catholic religion. This is clearly related in his conclusion:

"Wherefore defendant prays:

1. That the bonds of matrimony heretofore and now existing between plaintiff and defendant be dissolved and set aside,

and the parties hereto released from all obligations thereunder.

2. That the Court make such an order in the premises relative to the division of the property belonging to the defendant as to the Court may seem just and proper and the nature of the case may require.

3. For such further and other relief as to the Court may seem proper and the nature of the case may require."

This Answer and Cross Complaint was signed by Felix Pedro and notarized by James F. O'Brian on May 20, 1908.

Shann: On June 10, 1908, Mary attempted one last effort to obtain support with separate maintenance through the following motion presented through her attorneys, Farrell, Kane and Stratton:

"Comes now the plaintiff and moves this honorable court to enter an order herein striking from defendant's answer, his affirmative defense and cross-complaint, upon the ground and for the reason that said affirmative defense and cross-complaint are sham and frivolous; it appearing from the records and files of this cause that the same is untrue and that this court is without jurisdiction to grant the relief therein prayed. This motion is based upon the records and files of this cause."

Jim: Other than an order discharging the writ of attachment on Felix's property in Pierce County Washington (dated 28th day of December, 1911, over a year after Felix's death) nothing more is in the file. Apparently the two came to an agreement, and the couple began to live together, but Mary Pedro's aggressive character and attitude didn't seem to change. This was supported by Mullen, the Pedro family historian who suggests: "They apparently let the suit drop and returned to Fairbanks. Evidently Mary Ellen was a woman with her own way of dealing with opposition. The *Fairbanks Daily News-Miner* on June 15, 1909, reported that she was indicted on charges of assault with a deadly weapon at Honot Mine in conjunction with a pending lawsuit, Hanot vs. Pedro. In June 1910, Felix and Mary Ellen were enumerated together in the federal census in Fairbanks."

Massimo: Many of Felix's family members concluded from her statements that Mary was without a doubt only after his money. Seemingly she wanted money and property and separate maintenance, which would give her all the holdings when Felix died. In contrast, Felix wanted to share life with his wife, but recognizing that it was becoming futile he asked for a divorce. The way it was interpreted is that Mary saw that she might lose the "separate maintenance," and also the possibility that the divorce would separate her from Felix's money should he die. She knew well that he was in bad health and therefore she became amenable to a reconciliation.

Shann: It appears that they began to live together, although there doesn't seem to be any information regarding how they got along. Although, the incident at the Hanot Mine may be an indication that Mary was continuing her contrary ways. If I am permitted my own conclusion, it could be that Mary's aggressive and disruptive attitude led further to Felix's already poor health.

Jim: That is a possibility. Felix was having trouble with his heart as early as 1902 when he made the discovery on Pedro Creek. His health had not gotten any better over the years and while he and Mary were enumerated as living together in June of 1910, the following month July 22, 1910, Felix Pedro died.

Johne: While I was familiar with the date of his death, most of this story is new to me. I agree with what Jim said earlier. Mary's suit for separate maintenance provided a great deal of information about Felix Pedro that would never have been known. Memories fade and many times collecting accurate historical information is difficult. Without these court documents no one would know what actually happened.

Terrence: Exactly, especially where Felix is concerned. He was a little more shadowy. There have been a few surficial articles written about him but only a few with any depth. There is the other aspect as well, in Fairbanks history. Unlike Dawson or Nome where there were many chroniclers, in Fairbanks we only had maybe three at the most. In many cases the history is, as Johne pointed out, nothing more than faded memories. Whether memories or written words you never know which source to rely on, and even more difficult in Fairbanks history is that many of our sources are only a single source for many of the events. The information is impossible to double check. Even more difficult is when sources, as we have already seen in several cases, contradict each other. You just have to figure out which one is more reliable. Perhaps the most in-depth presentation was in Wickersham's book, *Old Yukon*. His account of Felix Pedro's life was focused on the discovery of gold in the Tanana Valley, and these court documents certainly provide a much clearer picture. Even so there are many gaps. Felix's desire for a solitary existence makes his life very difficult to research.

Jim: I agree, there were many gaps and of course more contradictions between sources. Some of these contradictions were centered around emotions. However, we do have the reported fact that Felix Pedro died on July 22, 1910, at the age of 52, exactly eight years after his discovery of gold on Pedro Creek.

Terrence: Yes, eight years to the day. Now that was an amazing coincidence—almost too amazing. Coincidences like that bother me. I did some research several years ago, and when I looked up the date of location of his claim on Pedro Creek in the recorder's office, I think it said July 25. Now that might have been the date he made the location not the actual date of discovery. There is an interesting research project here for some interested student.

Jim: I think you will agree that there are several research projects regarding Felix's life and travels. For example, it is surprising how many suggestions surfaced regarding Felix's death. One undocumented rumor has it that he was murdered by sticking a hat pin or needle into the base of his skull and into his brain. Another, reported October 15, 1972, in the Italian Newspaper, *Resto del Carlino*, translated by Mike Murray and reprinted by the *Fairbanks Daily News Miner,* July 21, 1984, states: "—In 1910 he did not feel good, they took him to the hospital. Next morning he was dead. The local stories go that he was poisoned."

Terrence: I have heard of some of those rumors, but lean toward the coroner's report that he died from heart disease brought on by overwork and the hardships of his many prospecting trips.

Jim: That is supported by an article presented by Bob DeArmond in the July 1968 issue of *Alaska Sportsman* which states: "Mr. Pedro had been bothered with heart trouble for some time and had been ill for several weeks before he entered St. Joseph's Hospital nearly two weeks ago.

Funeral services were conducted by Father Francis Monroe two days later at 10:30 am, Sunday, July 24, 1910, at the church of the Immaculate Conception." An interesting point is that Felix was held in such esteem by early day miners and residents that they flocked to the funeral in such numbers that many were unable to gain admittance to the overcrowded church.

Shann: Once again contradictions in stories surfaced. One source had Felix's age as 50 years old while another more accurately had it at 52. Felix, in his deposition on March 4, 1908, said, "I was born in Italy and am of the age of 49 years." Massimo reported that he was born on April 16, 1858. This would put him at 52 years old when he died. Regardless, the big question is, where was he buried? There is certainly some confusion surrounding this question.

Terrence: Yes there is, Shann. The obituary presented by Bob DeArmond clearly stated: "Interment will be in Holy Cross Cemetery in San Francisco." But there are questions.

Jim: Yes, I think one of the big questions brought out by Stan Patty, was that two days after the funeral it was reported that Felix would be buried in Holy Cross Cemetery, but the grave site, according to cemetery records, was not purchased by Mary Pedro until January 29, 1912.

Terrence: That is what I understood, Jim. The way Stan explained it, the plan was for the body to leave Fairbanks August 1, 1910, on the riverboat *Tanana* for Fort Gibbon, there to connect with the Yukon River sternwheeler *Susie* for the voyage to the port of St. Michael. Here is where the confusion begins; the shipment of the body beyond St. Michael was without documentation.

Shann: One other point that was particularly interesting was presented in Patty's article in the autumn issue of the 1971 *Alaska Journal*. He suggested that old-timers of the Fairbanks gold camp were to escort Pedro on the *Tanana* and that Mary's nephew Joe Doran was going to accompany the remains as far as Seattle. Mary was to stay behind to take care of legal details of the estate, then join her nephew in Seattle and take the body on to Holy Cross Cemetery in Colma, California.

Jim: The mystery is unclear. Following his research Stan Patty couldn't confirm if the "Plan" was followed. He suggests that some old-timers thought that Felix was not shipped out as planned but rather buried in Fairbanks before shipment to Colma. Regardless, there is an 18-month gap, between July 22, 1910, when he died, and January 31, 1912, when he was buried at Colma, during which the whereabouts of Felix Pedro's remains are unknown.

Shann: There are a lot of questions in addition to whether or not he was buried in the Pioneer Cemetery in Fairbanks before being shipped to Colma. Others to consider include whether his remains lay on a dock at St. Michael near the mouth of the Yukon River in Alaska or perhaps on some pier in Seattle, Washington, or possibly some warehouse on some San Francisco, California, dock. The lack of records create an overwhelming puzzle that may never be understood.

Jim: These are the most logical possibilities, but there are some much more deeply buried mysteries. It seems partially to hinge around the date he was interred at Holy Cross Cemetery, January 31, 1912. There is little question that Mary Pedro knew where Felix's body was at all times during that 18 month period. This is supported by the fact that she purchased the grave plot at Colma on January 29, 1912, just two days before Felix's remains were delivered. She purchased a plot of six graves for $283 with $100 down (she never paid the remainder). Only Felix was buried in that site and at a depth of six feet when he should have been buried at a depth of eight feet for double burial as suggested by the purchase contract. Now the big mystery: Felix had ties with Fanano in the province of Modena, Italy; state of Washington, United States; and Fairbanks in the Territory of Alaska in the United States. He had absolutely no known ties with San Francisco, California. Only Mary knew why Felix was to be buried in the Colma Cemetery. Only Mary knew why she purchased six plots rather than two, since there were no known relatives. Only Mary knew why he was buried at six feet rather than the agreed upon eight. Perhaps only Mary knew exactly where his body was for every minute of the previous 18 months. Perhaps in addition to what his friends suggested—that his health broke because of a bad heart developed over years of hardship and overwork on the gold trails—Mary's disrespect and poor treatment during his final two years was intended to hasten his death. The big question is, why wasn't he simply buried in the Fairbanks Pioneer Cemetery?

Shann: I see what you are driving at. Mary never had any respect for Felix. All she wanted was his money. She called him names and humiliated him in public. She attempted to get a legal separation with large monthly support payments. It seems that she wanted to keep the marriage because in the event of his death she would be the heir. When she saw that her attempt to get legal separation with support was failing and that Felix was leaning toward a divorce, she decided on reconciliation and began to live with him in Fairbanks. For several years before his death Felix was suffering with poor health, and if the past was any indication of how Mary treated him after they rejoined in Fairbanks, it is not hard to recognize that it may have contributed to his failing health. Mary's attitude and treatment of people is exemplified by her conviction of assault with a deadly weapon at the Hanot mine. No, I don't believe Felix had a happy relaxed home life after he and Mary reconciled their differences and decided to cohabitate in Fairbanks. In fact my perception is that he was probably miserable and this constant stress led prematurely to rapid deterioration of his health. It is not hard to conceive the thought that Mary, through emotional cruelty, led to Felix's early death.

Jim: Well Shann, I don't think that is something that we are going to find written so clearly in the literature, but it is an astute observation of facts and a possible conclusion. My thoughts are centered on Mary's feelings toward Felix. Seemingly she had nothing but contempt for him and, as you and Massimo have already pointed out, was only after his money. We have to keep in mind that Felix was extremely popular in Fairbanks. He was regarded as one of the best prospectors in the territory, and the miners in the Tanana Valley felt indebted to him for his discovery, which had led ultimately to their discoveries and private fortunes. Many of these people were illiterate workers who had never expected such success from life. It is possible that Mary hated the fact that Felix was held with such high esteem. During the funeral, which was held at 10:30 on Sunday, July 24, 1910, businesses were closed between 10 and 11 o'clock. So many of Felix's old friends and acquaintances attended the funeral that aisles within the church were filled to overflowing and lines of people were backed out the door and into the street, all out of respect for Felix Pedro's memory. Yes, Felix Pedro's body was dead, but he still lived on in the minds and hearts of the people of Fairbanks. It is quite possible that because of her overwhelming contempt for the little Italian from

Fanano, this infuriated Mary, and rather than burying him in the local Pioneer Cemetery she decided on Colma, California, where no one would visit the grave and he would be forgotten.

Shann: But as we now know he wasn't forgotten. There were several events leading up to Pedro's legendary status in Fairbanks. Some old-timers suggested that Pedro died destitute. This is highly unlikely, because he held several valuable mining claims either privately or in partnership with others. He may well have been low on cash, but his holdings were impressive for that period of time. One source suggested that he was worth over a $100,000, when a working man's wages were $1000 a year. Here is a possibility: perhaps he was low on cash when he died. In that case Mary would not have had the money to bury him. One source indicated that she sold all his holdings for $20,000, which was far below their actual value. One thought is that it took the 18 months to assemble the money and that during that time Pedro's remains did remain stored. Regardless, everything we have suggested is conjecture and the only person that knew the full story was Mary Ellen Pedro. She died in St. Joseph's Hospital in Fairbanks on May 20, 1930, after being hospitalized for almost a year. While there was some confusion regarding her age, she was about 70 and had resided in Fairbanks most of the time following Felix's death. The true story behind Felix Pedro's death, the mystery of the 18 months between his death and his burial, and the reason why he was interred in Holy Cross Cemetery in Colma, California, went to the grave with Mary Pedro on May 20, 1930.

Jim: While many "old-timers" remembered Felix with respect and honor, between the years of his death and 1952, memory of his contribution began to fade, although the Italian government continued interest. On July 22, 1952, the 50th anniversary of his discovery, two events stood out: The dedication of the Brooks Building on the University of Alaska campus and the unveiling of a monument on the Discovery Claim at 16 mile Steese Highway, in memory of Felix Pedro. I don't know how accurate this is, but I understand that the Italian government, as well as many Fairbanks residents, wanted the Brooks Building named after Felix Pedro, but the committee decided on Alfred H. Brooks because of his international recognition as a geologist who had performed significant work in Alaska. However, they did recognize the significance of Felix

Pedro's contribution to the founding of Alaska's "Golden Heart City" and as a result unveiled the monument that still stands at 16 mile Steese Highway in his memory. The short story behind the erection of that monument and the tribute to Felix is memorable. Pioneers of Alaska, Igloo #4 of Fairbanks selected a large granite boulder from Pedro Dome and set it up on the discovery site. Baron Felipo Muzi Falconi, the Italian consul general from San Francisco along with Alvaro Vito Beltrani, vice consul in Seattle, attended the celebration and provided a bronze plaque, courtesy of the Italian government, which was mounted on the boulder that now marks the Discovery claim 16 miles north of Fairbanks, the "Golden Heart City of Alaska." Falconi also presented a bust of Felix Pedro donated by the Italian government. The bust is currently on display in the University of Alaska Fairbanks museum.

Shann: To demonstrate how information can become distorted, such an astute investigator as Stan Patty confused the date of the 50th celebration, which was in 1952, with the first year of the Golden Days Celebration, which was in 1954. The events were clearly presented in a 1999 newspaper article by Dermot Cole. He points out that the 50th Anniversary of the gold discovery was in 1952 and that there was a big community celebration. The next year did not spark a big community celebration which was disappointing to *News-Miner* reporter Kay Kennedy. In Cole's article, Kennedy states, "Aside from putting a new wooden cross on Mrs. Pedro's grave, no one even put a candle on a bun to remember the city's birthday." Years later Kennedy recalled, "I thought something ought to be done about it." Kay Kennedy felt so strongly about it that she initiated discussions among Fairbanksans that led to the annual "Golden Days" festivities celebrating Felix Pedro's gold discovery, starting in 1954.

Terrence: Yes, and it was this event that would ensure that Felix Pedro would not be forgotten. It was also the event that sparked Stanton H. Patty's interest in tracing the whereabouts of Pedro's grave. Stan Patty, Ernest Patty's son and long time reporter for the *Seattle Times,* states, "Early in 1969 the trail led to the huge Holy Cross Cemetery in Colma...It took a considerable search by a cemetery official to find the exact site of Pedro's grave. A yellow file card provided clues to the section and row in the 110-acre cemetery with more than 275,000 graves." But Patty found that there was no monument for Pedro. Probing around through the thick grass bordered by large monuments, they discovered a small concrete block with the name "Pedro" etched in it apparently while the concrete was still wet. The cemetery official turned to Patty and said, "This is Mr. Pedro's grave. There is no doubt about it." The search for Felix Pedro had ended.

Jim: Patty's report regarding the discovery of Pedro's grave and the meager marking led Igloo #4 of the Pioneers of Alaska to consider placing a proper monument on the grave. They were informed that the balance of $183 would have to be paid before the monument could be placed. The article also sparked interest in Italy. Although Larry Barazzotto, the great grandnephew of Felix Pedro who visited the Golden Days celebration in 1999 said that his father had learned about Felix in 1977 when his cousin sent him a clipping from a New Jersey newspaper about the 75th anniversary of Fairbanks and Felice Pedroni, it seems that it was Patty's 1971 article that caught the interest of Pedro's 60-year-old niece in Italy, Ines Pedroni. Through the combined efforts of the notary Cortelloni and friends in the United States, they began the process of bringing Felix Pedro's body back to Italy for burial in Fanano. Interestingly, this all occurred as the members of Igloo #4 of the Pioneers were making arrangements to place a proper monument on Felix's grave. The cemetery superintendent wrote the Pioneers informing them that Pedro's remains would soon be disinterred and shipped to his home village in Italy. Felix Pedro's journey was not over. His body in death was as restless as he was in life.

Terrence: I remember, in my research, contacting the fellow in San Francisco who was in charge of exhuming Felix's body. He said, "Mr. Pedro is in a very good state of preservation." The restless remains of Felix Pedro were shipped to Fanano, Italy, in 1972, where, on October 12, he was buried for a second time, or perhaps a third time.

Jim: Yes, I had the privilege of visiting his grave site during the initial stages of this research in 2001. His remains now rest in a personalized vault.

Shann: That is appropriate for the man who discovered the first gold in the Tanana Valley. Today is July 22, 2002, and we are in the midst of the Centennial Celebration. We have scores of guests from Italy on hand to enjoy the festivities, in addition to scores of Felix's relatives from the

United States. Tell us about the sculpture presented to the City of Fairbanks by the people of Fanano, Massimo.

Massimo: Yes, on Saturday afternoon, Fairbanks Mayor Steve Thompson, Fanano Mayor Alessandro Corsini, and Graviano Pattuzzi, governor of the province of Modena, Italy unveiled the stone sculpture bestowed on Fairbanks by the people of Fanano. The four ton sculpture is titled "Il Ponte," which means "The Bridge." Fanano Mayor Alessandro Corsini spoke of the symbolism of the artwork: "We hope that this bridge will be for our citizens to come to your country and for your citizens to come to our country." In exchange, the city of Fairbanks presented the city of Fanano an imprint on moose hide of Felix Pedro panning gold. Pedro's descendants, Fanano residents, civic leaders and community band were accompanied by Fairbanks residents at the ceremony. The next event is this afternoon, when Jim will speak.

Jim: Thank you Massimo. That is correct. I have the privilege of giving the Centennial Rededication of Pedro's Monument, at the Discovery claim located at 16-mile Steese Highway at 2:00 p.m. this afternoon. It is a truly exciting honor and I am eagerly looking forward to it. Gentlemen, I want to thank you for joining with me today in this survey of Felix Pedro's life. It will be of great interest to others and add a fine chapter to the mining lore of Alaska.

Part IV

Earl Pilgrim

with
Jim Lounsbury
and
Leah Madonna

Jim Lounsbury
with
Jim Madonna
August 2001

Jim M.: Well this is a new adventure. Alaska Gold Trails has led us to a hardrock and placer mine on Eva Creek located on the south side of Ester Dome just 15 miles west of Fairbanks. We are visiting with Jim Lounsbury who's hobby is Fairbanks history, especially the history of the pioneers. Jim, tell us a little about yourself. Where were you born?

Jim L.: I was born in Fairbanks, Alaska, at St. Joseph's Hospital, in 1945.

Jim M.: Your father was born in Fairbanks as well, wasn't he?

Jim L.: Right. Actually he was born in Fox, October 12, 1910.

Jim M.: And your grandfather?

Jim L.: My grandfather came from Iowa to Oregon. He was attending the University of Oregon medical school. He fell in love and followed a young gal to Fairbanks in 1907. He married this young girl, Nellie Parsons, and they had their first child, which was my dad, on Engineer Creek, and that's where my dad grew up. He lived there from 1910 to 1913, and when E.T. Barnette embezzled all of the money out of Fairbanks, that broke my grandfather. He went back to Iowa. Of course, in 1913 my father was only three years old, so he went with him. When he was 18 years old and had 50 dollars in his pocket he hitchhiked to Seattle. He caught a boat to Alaska, returned to Fairbanks town where he was born, and spent the rest of his life here.

Jim M.: What year was that?

Jim L.: 1929 I think. He went to school at the University of Alaska in 1929, '30, '31 and '32 in Mining Engineering. He actually mined gold out at the F.E. Company (Fairbanks Exploration Company) property at Ester. We built a house there. There were four or five old partners that were running the drift up on a pup (small unnamed tributary) off of Eva Creek. It's about 15 miles from Fairbanks on Ester Dome.

Jim M.: Were they mining placer or hardrock gold?

Jim L.: They were mining placer at the time, but they got too old to work it, so my dad would come up on the weekend and help them. He acquired the property from them, built a cabin there, and that's where my wife, Lorna, and I are living now. In 1938 he ran a hardrock drift into the hill following a good-gold bearing quartz vein. He worked it until the war broke out. During World War II he couldn't buy powder, so he had to shut down. So that's that part of it. He kept the property, and last year we got a patent on it, signed by Babbitt.

Jim M.: Tell us a little more about the mining on Eva Creek.

Jim L.: Well, actually the F.E. Co. made one swipe with their bucket-line gold dredge on Eva Creek, turned and went out. They took $7 million worth of gold, out at the old price of $35 an ounce, in that one pass.

Jim M.: Is that right? That was at the mouth of Eva Creek, right?

Jim L.: That's at the mouth of Eva. Walt Wigger owns that ground now.

Jim M.: Did your grandfather know Felix Pedro?

Jim L.: Mmm...I don't know. He never said anything to me about it. He went back out to Iowa, and used to come up every five years or so, and I never did discuss it with him so I wouldn't know for sure.

Jim M.: Did he know E.T. Barnette?

Jim L.: I'm sure he did.

Jim M.: Did he ever talk about E.T. Barnette?

Jim L.: Well he did make a few remarks. I've got my great-grandfather's day-to-day diary in Fairbanks from 1905 all the way up to '32. He mentions my grandfather coming from Engineer Creek into town for E.T. Barnette's trial. That's how concerned he was over it. I thought that was interesting. He probably didn't know him as a friend.

Jim M.: Let's change direction here. You met this fellow that knew a lot about antimony ore, stibnite perhaps. Is that right?

Jim L.: Yes.

Jim M.: And his name was Earl Pilgrim. Where did you happen to meet Earl Pilgrim? How did that happen?

Jim L.: Well there was a lady named Magdeline Chassidy. She was an old-timer in Fairbanks, an old-time family. Her husband worked for the N.C. Company (Northern Commercial Company). He passed away. She knew Earl pretty well, and when he sold his mine at Stampede, he was interested in buying a cabin in Fairbanks. So she hooked us up with him. We had a cabin next door to the family home in Fairbanks. I bought my brother's interest in the family home, and we were partners on the house next door—the cabin was built by Ernie and Rudolph Johnson in 1945.

Jim M.: Did they used to call those guys Suit and Tie?

Jim L.: Suit and Tie, yeah that's right. They should have called them...

Jim M.: Coat and suit, maybe?

Jim L.: Yeah, something like that.

Jim M.: Were they Swedes?

Jim L.: Yeah, Ernie was mentioned in the book *Arctic Village* about Marshall Road. He was a guide for Bob Marshall. I knew both the guys when I was a kid. They used to buy my brother and me toys and stuff when we were kids. When they died they left the property to us kids. My brother sold it to Earl in 1980. He resided there from 1980 until 1984 when he moved into the Pioneer's Home.

Jim M.: Earl did?

Jim L.: Yeah, and he sold that house to another Earl who lives there right now. He is 97 years old. That's Earl Moratzka.

Jim M.: Is that right?

Jim L.: So we call that the House of Earls.

Jim M.: The House of Earls...and longevity.

Jim L.: Yes.

Jim M.: If you move into that house you have to hit at least 90.

Jim L.: Oh yes. Rudolph Johnson died there. He was 92. Earl Pilgrim 96, and now Earl Moratzka is 97.

Jim M.: Exactly where's that house?

Jim L.: Right next door to our family home, 214 Charles. It's on the register for historical buildings.

Jim M.: Where's that located exactly, Charles?

Jim L.: It's a block off of Minnie (Street). So if you went down Illinois Street, you'd turn by the Chevron station, drive down and go one block off of the Monroe (Catholic) School. That's a little white house there. It's a kind of unique place.

Jim M.: That's right, big history.

Jim L.: Oh yeah, big history.

Jim M.: I've got to drive by there just to take a look at it.

Jim L.: Yeah, I should take you over there and introduce you to the latest Earl.

Jim M.: Well okay, we're still back there where you met Earl. You were working at Healy, were you?

Jim L.: No, but when I was working down at the coal mines in Healy, I was interested in antimony. My father told me that if I wanted to learn about antimony, there was only one person in Alaska that could really tell me everything I needed to know, and that was Earl Pilgrim.

Jim M.: Did you know Earl at that time?

Jim L: No I didn't, and I always wanted to take that Stampede Trail over there and visit him. The end result was I made the last trip in with him to get his supplies, and when he passed away my brother and I flew over there and spread his ashes around his cabin. So I got to know him pretty well.

Jim M.: Tell us how you finally came to meet him.

Jim L.: Magdeline introduced us. He purchased the property, and I was living next door in the family home, so I spent a lot of time with him. I was about 35 years old, a fairly active and adventurous young man interested in mining, so Earl and I traveled all over the country together. We went to the state of Washington looking at mining property and even into Canada.

Jim M.: You and Earl became good partners didn't you?

Jim L.: Yeah, we were good sidekicks. We staked the Newsboy Mine back for him.

Jim M.: Tell us, when you first met Earl you just listened to his stories, is that it?

Jim L.: That's it. Well he asked me when he got settled into the cabin there he asked me "Who owns the Newsboy?" And I said "Well Earl, I really don't know but I'll look into it." So I did some research on it and learned that the area had just opened up for staking, so I got busy and went up and staked it for him. Actually, jointly we prospected it and on his 89th birthday I put a surprise cut in for him. Basically I did two things—I put a surprise cut in for him and I filled the original shaft up. He scared me once when he had me tie him onto a rope and lower him over that caved-in shaft, and I was just worried sick that something was going to happen to him. Here I was tied on the other end of the rope. You know, that was kind of a stupid move on my behalf. I got him out of there and I decided right then and there that was going to be corrected. So I took my earthmover up there on his 89th birthday and did a surprise cut to look for more values, and I also filled that hole in so that wouldn't happen again.

Jim M.: He took his first option on the Newsboy Mine according to the Fairbanks Alaska newspaper, on Tuesday, May 5, 1931. This is a quote: "Earl R. Pilgrim has taken an option on the Newsboy Mine and exploration work is being carried on in an effort to locate the vein beyond the fault." What you did was to make a cut across that fault and fill in the hole. What did he say when he saw that cut?

Jim L.: Well we didn't find anything.

Jim M.: Really, you didn't find the fault?

Jim L.: No we didn't find that fault. Actually it faulted at both ends of that shaft. A guy by the name of Hirshburger originally discovered that, and according to the old reports on it he took one truckload of ore down to the China mills. He melted down one gold block. Based on that one truckload of ore and that one gold brick, he sold 100,000 shares of stock in 24 hours in Fairbanks in 1911. It was a big thing. They set a stamp mill up there and ran it for a while and they got down to the 250-foot level. When Earl took that over in 1931 he went down there to the 250-foot level and he drilled and shot a round (blasted the rock) and he got into some real nice ore, and he said he hit every other rung coming up out of there, he was so happy. Then he went down and shot another round and it was gone. It was just a small pocket.

Jim M.: Advancing forward in time to when you made the cut, where did you go from there?

Jim L.: Well we did a little backhoe work and we put another crosscut in but we didn't find anything. That is as far as we went. Earl Beistline always expressed interest in that property. He mentioned it to us a couple of times, probably because he had adjoining property. And when Earl had his leg amputated from infection, in the Pioneers Home I knew we weren't going to do anything more with it and the only reason I was holding it was because of Earl. So we worked an arrangement out for Beistline to get that ground. He owns it right now, and I think it's part of that connection with the True North deposit—it's in that area—so I think he is working with those guys. So it is going to continue to be developed, which was our interest.

Jim M.: Tell us some stories you know about Earl. Start with the guard up at the Stampede Mine—Mr. Grunt.

Jim L.: Mr. Grunt was a martin—a pet martin.

Jim M.: How did it become a pet?

Jim L: Earl was friends with all animals in the country. He even had a black bear that was visiting his place, and his meat kept disappearing out of his cache and he couldn't figure out how it could happen, because it was latched all the time. Then one day he opened up the door, and Susie the black bear had steaks in both her arms. She was taking off with his meat but he told me she was relatching the door. She was tricking him. But this Mr. Grunt was a very interesting critter. He would follow Earl to the adit in the morning and Earl would work all day in the tunnel, and in the evening when he would come out that martin would be sitting there waiting for him. One day Earl's mom fell and bruised her hip in Seattle and he had to make a special trip out there, and he was gone for a couple of weeks. When he got back to Stampede his cabin looked like Swiss cheese. It had holes all through it. He thought about it and thought about it and said to himself, "Hmmm, Mr. Grunt what am I going to do about this?" They are like a bears they never go out the same hole they come in. He had augured his way into the cabin looking for Earl because he missed him. He didn't see him so he augured his way back out. A few days passed, then he would augur his way in another hole and augur his way out. After two weeks of him being absent Earl's cabin looked like Swiss cheese. Earl wasn't upset, he understood the nature of the beast. I don't know what ever happened to Mr. Grunt, but I've got a picture sitting right here of Earl sitting in his cabin, and I did have one someplace of Mr. Grunt actually feeding right out of Earl's mouth, but I don't know what happened to it.

Jim M.: Is that right? That would be an interesting photo to share.

Jim L.: I might have given it to George then it ended up at the University. I don't know. Anyway, that's one of the stories of Earl. Over the years I traveled around with him, we went up to Wiseman and spent time with Harry Leonard, and prospected on the way up. We found an outcropping of quartz vein at Baker Mountain. We went down and looked at some mining property in Canada…at Dominion Creek and Quartz Creek, which is held by my wife's family.

Jim M.: What year was that?

Jim L.: That was about '81…yeah, '81 is when we went down there, and that's where I met my wife.

Jim M.: Oh, is that right?

Jim L.: She was working at Boundary for Action Jackson, cooking for them, and Earl and I were going to look at some mining property with my wife's cousin. This Harold Schmidt, he did a lot of things in the Fortymile country in his time. He mined on Jack Wade Creek, and he was a partner on that dredge that sits alongside the road. He had four partners. My wife could probably tell you better than I can. They're all mining engineers, and they tried to go up Jack Wade Creek with that dredge and it was too steep. He was the only one that knew that. He told those guys, "Whatever you do, don't try going up there. This is too steep a grade for a dredge." It didn't make it, and that's where it ended up-stuck there.

Jim M.: That was the Jack Wade Dredge. It wasn't the Chicken Dredge?

Jim L.: No, it was Jack Wade. It is kind of a famous dredge. There's lots of pictures of that one over the years. Anyway, this Harold Schmidt had some equipment, and we went and looked at it. Then Earl and I made a trip down to Eastern Washington looking at some mining property my dad was interested in years and years ago. My brother, Lloyd, in Seattle, found out there was a lady in a nursing home that owned that ground. It was patented, and she was willing to sell it. So, Earl and I were willing to look at it. So we flew to Seattle. We took my brother's van, and we drove over to this little town called Loomis. It's right at Palmer Mountain there. During World War I, they were running a drift through the hill. It was a government-funded project, and they were looking for copper. There was a shortage of copper at the time. They went through some quartz veins that were gold-bearing. They just went right by 'em and my dad knew this. That's why he had such an interest in this ground. Here it became available, and, of course, he had passed away. Earl and I were chomping at the bit. We got there, and it was just a one-horse town. I'm not superstitious, but something inside me said this wasn't for us. There was a restaurant and a service station. I went into the restaurant and I asked this person there, "Where's the adit to this mine?" He pointed to the service station. I said, "No, that's the service station." He says, "Behind it." I walked out and looked behind it, and sure enough, there was an old adit there. It was all fenced in. So I went back and said, "Well how can I get into this property to look at it?" He said, "Well you have to go down the street about a quarter mile and there is a mailbox there, and you drive up the driveway, and that fellow has the grazing rights to this property. He'll get you a key and you can go in and look at it." Earl and I drove up there with my brother, and looked at that mailbox and it had my name on it, first and last, Jim Lounsbury. I said, "Earl, this isn't for us. Let's get outta here." We turned around and left.

Jim M.: Is that right? You didn't even go into the mine?

Jim L.: I never did, but I did call the guy. Later on, I bought some property in Sand Point, Idaho. My wife and I would drive out there quite often and play around on the property. I thought I would take that route by that mine again and call him. I called up and he was in Florida. He had some property in Florida that had suffered some storm damage and he was out there taking care of it. His caretaker was there and I told him the story of how I almost got to talk to him to view the property. It just spooked me to have my name on a mailbox. Someday, maybe I'll get down there. I think it would be fun to talk to him.

Jim M.: Do you plan on going into that mine?

Jim L.: Yeah. I guess I probably should've went right up and talked to the fellow and told him who I was.

Jim M.: Earl would have loved it.

Jim L.: He probably would have. I probably should've followed through on it. That was just one thing. Earl and I traveled around the country and did a lot of things over the years. He was a prince of a guy. Perfect role model for a young miner to follow in the footsteps of, or try to.

Jim M.: Tell us a few more stories about Earl. Tell us the story about his escapade with the folks who bought the Stampede Mine.

Jim L.: Yeah, you were at that big to-do. It was the graduating banquet for the University Mining Engineers and I am trying to think what year that was...early '80s, and this fellow Ed Dole had purchased the property from Earl, and his nephew was there, and they'd just signed the papers. He promised Earl that he would replace some timbers in the adit, and get right after the mine. Soon as he signed the papers in a loud voice he said, "There's nothing in the ground. It's worthless." So he turned it over to the University and later, through D2, somehow the Park Service got involved. Anyway, Earl knew he'd been shafted then.

Jim M.: Well Earl was under the impression that Dole was going to work the mine. All Earl wanted was for the mine to be worked. Is that correct?

Jim L.: Yes. He wanted it developed. The University part was good, but the Park Service was questionable, and it ended up being a bad deal. The mine buildings literally got blown up and it was a horrible fiasco.

Jim M.: Tell us about the blowup, but first tell us about what happen to Earl at the party.

Jim L.: Okay, that was a good one. This Ed Dole had the press there with him with their big fancy cameras, and he was running around with his hand sticking straight out trying to catch up with Earl to get this famous promotional picture for what he was going to do, and Earl caught wind of what was going on, and Leah, your wife, was tipped off on it. So she took Earl out on the floor dancing, and they danced for, I'll bet, 45 minutes around that place. They stayed just one step ahead of Ed Dole. It was just a comical thing to see.

Jim M.: And Dole was frustrated?

Jim L.: Yep, and Earl was fuming.

Jim M.: Here he was with a young, beautiful woman and he wasn't even enjoying himself. He was fuming about Dole too much. What a shame.

Jim L.: Finally, the music stopped, and he was cornered. The cameras were there and Ed had his hand straight out and Earl had his arms straight down like he was standing at attention in formation. He wouldn't shake that guy's hand on a bet.

Jim M.: Tell us how the mine got blown up.

Jim L.: I'm not really sure exactly what went on, but they claimed the mill building was so tight that dust caused the explosion. Well, I made the last trip in with Earl to get his personal belongings when he sold it, and I walked into that mill building and there was daylight. There were big openings. There was no possible way there could be tight air-dust problems in that building. Anyway, they blew the mill building up and it blew tin all over the side of the hill. It blew his supply building off of its foundation, across the valley, and expensive drills were laying out on the ground. Everything was just littered. It looked like a bunch of bums had been living there, and they just left it that way. I just could not believe it.

Jim M.: Was there some dynamite in the building? That's the story I'd got. There was dynamite and they ignited the dynamite.

Jim L.: Well, I think there was some. They would have been better off if they had just burnt it off. That is all they would have had to do, but I think someone wanted to make the big explosion.

Jim M.: They simply wanted to see something blow up.

Jim L.: That's probably what they wanted to do, and it's just a shame. Dynamite's a wonderful tool for moving rock, and that's all it's good for as far as I'm concerned, but somebody had a different idea. It just left a mess. The bad thing is that they didn't clean it up, and I didn't have the heart to tell Earl what happened. He was still alive. I knew it would kill him if he was told about it, so I kept it a secret.

Jim M.: He was in the Pioneers Home at that time?

Jim L.: Yes. I really didn't want him to hear that news.

Jim M.: Some things are better left unsaid aren't they?

Jim L.: Right, but he's a spiritual type guy, and his ashes are spread around his cabin. I made sure of that, and if his spirits are in the right direction, his enemies better stay away from there. Make sure it's nice and tidy, nobody better make any bad errors over there.

Jim M.: Tell us the story about when he went to a meeting with James Watt with you. Wasn't that the only time in a couple of decades that you put on a suit?

Jim L.: Yeah, I put on a suit when I graduated from high school, but I didn't wear one after that because I was mining and moving dirt. It just don't match. Earl was invited to James Watt's luncheon at Westmark— Traveler's Inn at that time. The day before that, Frank Murkowski had a deal for Watt, and Earl was invited, and I went along as kind of his bodyguard and friend. So I bought a suit. Suited up for it, and the next day we went to the luncheon and there was a demonstration outside the door. Actually, they brought it inside. There were people in little bunny suits bouncing around and giving Watt a little trouble. So we walked outside the door.

Jim M.: I remember what Watt said there. He said, "I'm glad to see this, because in America we can do this kind of thing." I thought that was the wisest thing he could've said. It quieted people down, and he went on with his presentation.

Jim L.: Earl did something that kind of rocked my heels a little bit.

Jim M.: How old was he?

Jim L.: Earl was 90 years old. We walked out and were standing on the intersection ready to walk across the street and this young man had a sign "I'm an Alaskan for Alaska," and he was waving it in front of Earl.

Jim M.: Were you and Earl alone?

Jim L.: There was one little female police officer standing right next to us. Earl just kind of smiled at this fellow, and he coaxed him over, used his finger, begging him to come over. He got right up close to Earl. Earl just took that sign and pulled that right up to him, chest to chest. It threw the guy off balance, and Earl just jammed him in the gut as hard as he could with his fist and pushed him out into the street. The guy crashed right into the asphalt.

Jim M.: Did it knock the air out of him?

Jim L.: Knocked the air totally out of him, and he was gasping. I looked over at this little female officer and she was grinning from ear-to-ear because that's what she wanted to do to every one of those guys I'm sure. I look around like, "Does anyone want to continue this argument?" Nobody did, so Earl and I walked off. Man, I was so proud of him. If I ever make 90, and that situation would ever arise, I hope I will do the same thing.

Jim M.: There's only one thing worse than getting in a fight with a senior citizen isn't there. It's getting your butt whipped by a senior citizen!

Jim L.: (Snicker) Yup, that's exactly what happened there! Oh, that was fun. It didn't hurt the guy; it was just Earl's way of making a statement.

Jim M.: Do you have any more stories about Earl you would like to share?

Jim L.: I have plenty. That same year, on his 90th birthday, the Roaring Jazz Express was put on by the Resource Council in Anchorage, and they lined up all of the passenger cars on the Alaska Railroad, and in between those they put freight cars. In those freight cars, they put roulette wheels, and they had three brass bands on this train. Over 400 people entered this thing, and it happened to be on Earl's birthday, his 90th birthday. I went down with him, and they told me they were going to have a lady jump out of a cake. I just took it with a grain of salt and said, "Okay." On the way down there, there was this lady all decked out in furs sitting right across, kitty-corner, from Earl on this train just eyeballing him. I couldn't figure out how she fit in. She wasn't with anybody, but she was there. Anyhow, we got down there and everybody got in a big circle, there was 400 of them. Steve McAlpine came out to the podium and gave a speech about Earl's 90th birthday, the guest of honor, "and now Earl we're going to present you with your present." So this lady sitting there with all of these furs came out, carrying a little box. She set it up on the podium and turned it on. It was a cassette recorder, and it was burlesque music, and she cranked that thing up. Professional dancer, unbelievable, danced around there, and then all of a sudden, the furs began disappearing. It was flying everywhere. She got down to one piece of fur, and she threw that over Earl's head, and was doing the hoochie-coochie, and Earl was dancing away there kind of a little blushed, not too bad. Man, I thought he was going to have a heart attack and die on me—90 years old. Magdaline came along. That was the lady who introduced him to me at the cabin next door to the family home. I thought she was going to have a heart attack, but she was grinning from ear-to-ear. Then McAlpine said, "If any of you ladies in this audience would like to dance with Earl, please step forward." There were about 14 of them lined up. He danced with every one of them— fox-trot, the whole works; all of that old music. He just burnt up the dance floor. It was quite a test on the old guy, but he was in good form.

Jim M.: The first one got his heart pumping, the rest of them just carried him through.

Jim L.: Just carried him through. It was great. It was quite a deal. Probably the only other thing that I could think of right now is this one painting that I have of this mule on the wall here. It was a painting done by Katie Burk. It was Dick Mackey's daughter-in-law. It's a picture of a white mule and a bunch of dogs standing around waiting, and this dog bowl with caribou bones in it, and they're waiting for seconds. This picture was done because of a story told by Earl when he first went into Stampede. He rented a mule from the Park Service. On the way in they shot a caribou for camp meat. They gutted it and left it lying on the ground with the legs up and the carcass open. It'd rained that night and the water collected in it. The next morning, they got ready to leave, and that caribou had quite a bit of water in the carcass, and that mule just reached in there and sucked that water out of that carcass, and left a ring of blood around its nose. They all looked at each other, "What do we have here?" So they threw the carcass on the mule and on the way in, every once in a while, that mule would reach around and grab a chunk of raw meat off it. Later, when they would cook caribou steaks at night, they would lay the caribou leftovers in this doggie bowl and give it to the mule. The mule would eat what it wanted, and the dogs got what was left over, and that's what this painting was about.

Jim M.: Did Earl tell you any more like that one?

Jim L.: I know there were a lot of other ones, but I really can't think of a lot of them offhand. He told me one time—I think it was the time he went to Seattle to visit his mom, when she bruised her hip—his dad had sent him a box-and-a-half of cigars and told him to quit smoking. Well, after dinner, his dad lit up a cigarette. Earl said, "Dad, I thought you told me to quit smoking. You sent me those cigars." "After 80-odd-some years, son, it's hard to quit." But his dad lived until he was 98, I think. He had a prostate operation. After he got out of the hospital, he was lying down on the sofa. He got up to hoe the garden, and he shouldn't have. An incision broke internally and he bled to death. So otherwise, who knows how long he would've lived. He was going good, but he had to have that operation.

Jim M.: It wasn't a normal death was it? That is why, during his interview, Earl said his father's death didn't count when calculating family longevity. Give us some details; where was Earl born?

Jim L.: Earl was born in Durango, Colorado, in 1896.

Jim M.: He did a lot for Alaska and had a very full life. Did he die here?

Jim L.: Yes, he died here. He was 96 when he passed away. Yes, he was quite the guy. He supplied antimony for World War II, the Korean conflict, the Vietnam conflict, and then to show their gratitude the Park Service blew the doggone place up.

Jim M.: Mining was in Earl's blood wasn't it, Jim?

Jim L.: Yes it was, from the early beginning to the end, all Earl ever wanted to do was go mining. He would say, "The only fun thing in life was mining."

Jim M.: Well he certainly made a name for himself in Alaska's mining history and contributed to the development of the country. Thank you for the interview, Jim; you're always interesting to talk to. You're just full of historical information. Hope we can do it again sometime.

Leah Madonna
with
Jim Madonna
April 22, 1988

Jim: Good afternoon folks. This is Jim Madonna on Alaska Gold Trails. We've got a fascinating program for you today. But before we start, we've got some good news and we've got some bad news. The good news is that I've got a guest that is above all guests, in my view. Today, our guest is Leah Madonna, the owner of Alaskan Prospectors. The bad news is that I have been accepted into the Ph.D. program at an Australian university and as a result, it looks like the Alaska Gold Trails show might be coming to the end of the trail here very soon. Let's get back to the good news. Welcome to Alaska Gold Trails, Leah.

Leah: Thank you, Jim. It is great to be here.

Jim: We already have a caller. Hi you're on the air.

Caller: This is Jesse Atencio.

Jim: Jesse, you keep calling this program all of the time. You sure have a lot of questions. Maybe we should have you on the show.

Caller: Okay, as long as you have Leah there to protect me and answer some of my questions.

Jim: Do you have a question you would like to ask her now?

Caller: Yes I would.

Jim: Leah, Mr. Atencio has a question for you. Go ahead with your question, Jesse.

Caller: You sell Garrett metal detectors at Alaskan Prospectors. Like a lot of other people, I am very interested in metal detectors, and I would like to hear some success stories some of your customers have had. I think a lot of people would like to hear more about that. Some of the perception I get from people who talk to me is that these metal detectors are magic boxes, and you have to have a degree in witchcraft to use them. If you can explain the way they work a little bit, I think a lot of people would benefit from it.

Jim: Jesse, I think we'll fade into that during the program, so stay tuned, and we'll give you a full report on some of the success stories. I'm sure Leah has a number of them.

Caller: Alright, thank you.

Jim: Thanks for the call Jesse. Leah, let's get some background. When did you first come to Alaska?

Leah: In the mid-1950s Jim; I'm an old-timer up here.

Jim: That means you're a pioneer, probably over 30 years in the state.

Leah: Right.

Jim: And you now own a store called Alaskan Prospectors. Is that correct?

Leah: That is correct.

Jim: Tell us a little about what you sell over there and what types of services you have in the store.

Leah: Well, we sell mostly mining equipment, but we also have Alaskan gifts for the visitor. We have rocks, minerals, beautiful crystals from all over the world, gold pans, sluice boxes, Alaskan books, mining books and how-to-do-it type books.

Jim: Where are you located, Leah?

Leah: In the "Ugly" Quonset Hut there on College Road. That's 504 College Road.

Jim: I see. You know, we were just talking about the activities that were occurring in and around Fairbanks, or coming up pretty soon. Isn't there an activity coming up in the middle of the summer. And Jesse asked the question regarding metal detectors. Isn't there a metal detecting jamboree occurring in the state in the middle of the summer people might like to know about?

Leah: Well, I can't confirm that particular event, but there is a metal-detecting contest I believe, scheduled at Paradise Valley on the 21st of June. Of course, that's up to the miner and the completion of his plans. In addition to that, in the fall, during the Palmer Fair, there is now an annual metal detecting contest.

Jim: So there are a couple of contests going on. We'll get into metal detecting in just a few minutes. Leah, you also pointed out that you sell a large variety of equipment over in your store, and right now we have a call. So let's see what the folks have to say here. Hi, you're on the air.

Caller: Yeah, I just wanted to know if you know of anyone who has gotten their wetlands permit? I've gotten several calls asking me. Do you know of any miners that might have gotten them so far?

Jim: Wetlands permits? Is this Doris?

Caller: Yes.

Jim: Doris, we get the quarterly Army Corps of Engineers publication through the University. They have been sent out and a number of people have gotten their permits, but you know I'm a little hesitant to make comment on that kind of thing, because sometimes I make an error. It doesn't happen very often, but every once in awhile it happens, but I'll tell you who to call. It's in Anchorage, of course. The number is 353-7062, and that's the U.S. Army Corps of Engineers down there and they'll give you real accurate information on that, and then you don't have to say Jim told you so, okay?

Caller: Do you get these publications? Where do you get these publications?

Jim: They just send them automatically once they are requested.

Caller: Out of Anchorage?

Jim: Yes, to the University. I'm sure if you wanted, they would put your name on the mailing list. The publication comes right to the School of Mineral Engineering at the University. If you call the Mining Extension office between 9 and 1 o'clock, I have immediate access to that information. The number is 474-7702.

Caller: 474-7702. That's strictly Monday through Friday, right? From 9 until 1, right?

Jim: Yes, 9 to 1 someone is always in the office.

Caller: Well okay. Thank you, Jim.

Jim: Thank you, Doris. Bye. Okay Leah, where were we? We were talking about some of the things you have over there at Alaskan Prospectors, but like Jesse asked, what brand of metal detectors do you sell?

Leah: I sell the Garrett, White and Fisher lines of metal detectors. There's something interesting in selling these detectors as well, Jim. We have a Sourdough Theater in Alaskan Prospectors, and I have a nice inventory of video tapes on using the detectors as well as other small-scale mining equipment. Customers are welcome to come over and view these at no charge.

Jim: How many people can you accommodate in the theater?

Leah: The theater can hold between 1 and 16 people. As a matter of fact, during the summer months, visitors who come into Alaska are invited in and we show them a short—about a 10-or 15-minute little short historical Alaskan mining film. It's just a little added attraction for the visitor.

Jim: We have another call, Leah. Hi, you're on the air.

Caller: Hello Jim. This is Phil here, from out in North Pole.

Jim: Hi Phil.

Caller: Hi, how ya' doin'?

Jim: Fine.

Caller: Say I got a question for you on metal detectors. We're going to have some relatives coming up from Outside this summer. My brother-in-law expressed an interest in metal detectors, to do a little panning and gold prospecting. I used to be a miner myself. I never used a metal detector though; we used heavy equipment. I wonder if you could tell us a little about what kind of range they have, and what a good model would be. Can you help us out on that?

Jim: Sure, Phil, we'll just let Leah go over the different kinds of detectors and how they work and their range and so forth right now.

Caller: Okay, I'll hang up and listen, Jim.

Jim: Thanks for the call Phil.

Caller: You're welcome.

Jim: Okay Leah, I think you got the question. Why don't you tell us a little bit about the different models of metal detectors.

Leah: Certainly, Jim. There's a complete price range in detectors, and they're equally efficient. Some are geared to gold prospecting more than others.

As an example, there's the Garrett Gold Hunter, which has really come into it's own. It's a mid-price-range unit. It is electronically tuned to gold, while other models are more sensitive to treasures of a different type, such as coins. In the store we have a replica of the largest gold nugget ever taken with a metal detector anywhere in the world, and that was the Hand of Faith nugget from Australia, which weighed 874 troy ounces. The interesting thing about the detectors today though is not how large a nugget they will detect. Probably any detector would detect large nuggets. The value of the gold detector is the small particles they can detect. Even particles as small as a match head lying near the surface or just a few inches under the soil can be detected with this new Garrett detector. There's been quite a bit of success in Alaska with these units. Many of you may have read last year of a couple of visitors who came to Alaska—Grace and Otis Rude—who came up to see our state, and then they made a trip up to Paradise Valley for two days. Now this was at a professional mine; however, in one day's time, Otis Rude took out 19 gold nuggets with his Garrett Gold Hunter, the largest being over five-and-a-half ounces. The smallest was down about one pennyweight, the thumbnail size or something in that range. This was very interesting because Otis is hard of hearing, and of course, he had his earphones tuned up very high. People up and down the creek could hear the sound going off on this nugget. By the way, he used a seven-and-a-half inch coil, which is the standard size coil, not the large one. This large nugget was taken at two-and-a-half feet of depth.

Jim: Well Otis was one of the big success stories in the state. We have a call. Hi, you're on the air. Do you have a question?

Caller: I'm an oldtimer, that is, a longtime resident here. Fortunately or unfortunately, depending on how you look at it, I just never had gold fever, but I have been asked many times, by tourists, when they have these detectors, where do you tell them to go? They always want to know. I'm usually kinda stumped on that one. She mentioned a place a couple had gone called Paradise Valley. I have no idea where that is, but they do eventually ask you that question, "Where can I go to pan gold?" Those who just don't want to go to another tourist trap for a demonstration or whatever.

Jim: Well, I think there's some places that have been set aside specifically for gold panning and recreational mining. I'll let Leah handle that question. Leah, where is Paradise Valley?

Leah: Okay, Paradise Valley is a private, commercial miner's operation in the Brooks Range, and he does open it to recreational mining for a certain number of visitors. There is a fee involved, but it is certainly a rewarding place; many people have gotten gold, including large nuggets, up there. I don't think anyone has come home empty-handed. On the other hand, BLM has set aside a lot of land where you can do recreational panning, sluicing, dredging, and of course, you can use the metal detector. We must remember, the metal detector is something that can be used along the tailings piles and along the rivers when you're out fishing. You can check on it, but there is nothing wrong with being up on the Chena fishing, and one of the family members out playing with the detector and perhaps becoming lucky. There has been gold found in the Chena, from old reports I've read. This would apply all over the state, unless, of course, there is some restriction like in a national park. I would like to add that these detectors are not that complicated to use. Certainly anyone, including the visitor who stops and camps along our road systems, would find many places to use a detector. Many of the prospectors that buy these detectors have talked about going around the tailing piles, along the Chatanika, in different places, of course not on private land. I hope that answers your question.

Caller: It sure does. Great, appreciate it. Thank you.

Jim: Well, thank you for the call. We gave quite a bit of time to the metal detectors. Perhaps we should talk a little bit about the other equipment. What other kind of recreational equipment do you have for the weekend prospector?

Leah: Gold pans, sluice boxes, and of course, little suction gold dredges. So what would you like to know about them?

Jim: Well, what kind of gold pans are there? I was at the recent placer mining conference and I heard you speak about high-impact plastic. What's that all about?

Leah: They are fantastic!

Jim: They are?

Leah: One thing that is nice about the plastic pan is that it's available in many colors, Jim, and prospectors can do all kinds of things with plastic that they can't do with steel. First of all that plastic pan doesn't rust.

Secondly, as we get older, we find that our eyes are a little dimmer, and the gold gets a little more hard to see in that old rusty steel pan. So plastic pans are great. The black sand and the gold shows up real fast.

Jim: I see, and do you still have the traditional steel pan?

Leah: Absolutely. It wouldn't be a prospecting store and not supply what the miner wants. We have anything in a pan from one-inch up to about 17-inch and larger by special order.

Jim: Didn't I see a 36-inch pan in there at one time?

Leah: Yes, but it's a little bit difficult to pan with. We really recommend that to the artists who want to make the super painted pan.

Jim: I see. Look, I just want to tell the folks out there, who are listening, that we are here with Leah Madonna, from Alaskan Prospectors, who is the supplier of the mining and prospecting equipment here in Fairbanks, Alaska. If you would like to talk to her about some of this equipment or anything about gold mining or gold prospecting, give us a call here at Alaska Gold Trails at 479-TALK. That's 479-8255. Leah, you were saying that you had some gold dredges over there. Tell us about these gold dredges. How big do they get.

Leah: Well, the recreational dredges start at a little two-inch dredge that weighs about 38 pounds, and it's called the Backpacker. It's a nice dredge to work with on weekends. The wife and kids like to use it as much as the husband. Suction dredges range in size from two-inch up to eight-inch. For those who are not familiar with suction dredges, let me explain what the significance of those numbers is. First a two-inch dredge is capable of processing gravel up to two inches in diameter whereas an 8-inch dredge is capable of processing gravel up to eight-inches in diameter—the larger the dredge the more gravel it will process, and hopefully the more gold will be recovered. As you might expect, an eight-inch dredge is pretty big and it's not a weekend model. It's something for the more serious, small-scale miner. A lot of people want a transition between a gold pan and a gold dredge. That would be the portable sluice box. They are for those who want something they can just throw in their car and take out when they go fishing, and try for a little gold at the same time.

Jim: That's pretty nice. Let me ask a few questions. You mentioned that you had crystals from around the world. You have rocks from around the world. I noticed on the sign there it says, "Alaskan Gifts." What kind of nice things do you have that a Fairbanksan might like to send or take as a gift to someone outside?

Leah: We manufacture an Alaskan Mineral Card, which has specimens, labeled and in a picture frame so it can be hung on a wall or displayed. Also, as you might guess, we have Alaskan Canned Gold-Bearing Gravel, which is a nice gift to take Outside if you want to do a little panning when you get back home.

Jim: Ah, we have a call. Welcome to Alaska Gold Trails, you're on the air.

Caller: This doesn't really have anything to do with Alaska, but Leah, please, tell us about your opals.

Leah: Okay. Those are my pet rocks. I brought them back from Lightning Ridge, Australia. I would like to find a good home for them, of course, but we have probably one of the best selections of the Lightning Ridge Black Opal in the state. We have a complete price range. We have triplets, solids and doublets. These were bought direct from the miner; they're not through jewelry stores or outlets. We do have a nice supply of those.

Jim: How's that? Did that answer your question? Hello? I guess they hung up. Leah, give us kind of a rundown. When walking through the front door of your shop, what is a person going to see? Take us right through to the back end where all of the equipment is.

Leah: When you walk through the door, you're going to be surrounded by books, minerals and crystals. After that, you're going to see a lot of pictures hanging on the wall of mining and prospecting, kangaroos, emus from Australia. Then, we go along to the gold pans. We have a gold-pan wall. I don't think you could walk out of there without finding the proper size that you might desire. As you go back a little further, you come to sluice boxes and pumps. Of course, we have the accessory parts for those gold dredges too. There's a lot of little pieces sitting around. Then there are the gold-concentrating wheels that separate the gold from the black sand. Those come in any size, from a tiny unit in a tub that could be used right out at the stream, to something that would be used at home or at the mine. A little past that we run into the Sourdough Theater, where we would welcome all Alaskan visitors and newcomers to Alaska to visit and view a short little <u>free</u> film on the mining history of the North. If you want to know more about equipment, we would be happy to show you our videos.

Jim: How about out in the yard. What kind of yard display do you have?

Leah: It's history. Besides some little displays—I'll call them cabin-style shelters for our larger suction dredges—there are all kinds of old mining equipment. We have a complete replication of the bucket line-dredge mining that was being conducted in the Fairbanks area between 1928 and 1960. We begin with the churn drill then the hydraulic monitor, followed by thaw points, and finally we have the working miniature model of a bucket-line gold dredge. All of this is in the state of being set up. In addition we have a stamp mill and ore cars. Oh! Also we have a complete drift mine set up, including boiler, steam engine and highliner. It is exactly the way the old-time drift mining operations had these things set up.

Jim: Anything else?

Leah: Yes, we have some classic cars for our customers viewing. In addition, there are lots of little things around the yard such as wheelbarrows, steam points and ore cars. Of course we have gold panning for our customers.

Jim: Don't you have an authentic log cabin?

Leah: Oh yes, but that is Edral Smith's cabin. He stays there when he is in town and not out prospecting and mining. He is one of the true pioneers that came across the Chilkoot in 1898. I just don't know how he keeps going at his age.

Jim: Do you have anything else for us, Leah?

Leah: I can only invite all those people who are interested in these kind of historical things to come out and take a look. I should add that we have a beautiful mineral display in the shop and all this viewing is free to our customers. We enjoy having people come in and look at the collection of minerals and antiques. There is so much more than what I have told you. It is surprising what you might find inside an "Ugly" Quonset Hut.

Jim: Leah, before our trail comes to an end here, let's change directions and get to one of your more recent activities. Didn't you interview Earl Pilgrim?

Leah: Yes, Jim Lounsbury and I interviewed Earl a few years ago.

Jim: How did it go?

Leah: Oh, it was wonderful. That man has had one of the most interesting lives of anyone I know. When it comes to prospecting, mining and adventure, he did it all.

Jim: Did you take lots of notes?

Leah: No, the interview was taped. Two full cassette tapes.

Jim: I understand that some day you, Jim Lounsbury and I will get together and present Earl Pilgrims life story. Is that correct?

Leah: Yes, but there is a little personal story that probably won't be in the book, that you and your audience might be interested in.

Jim: Let's hear it.

Leah: Well first there is some background you should know. First, Earl wasn't a big man. In fact he was not much taller than me and I am five feet two inches. The second was that Earl first came to Alaska to teach at the University. He left a few years later with a great deal of bitterness toward the college. In short, he was not a friend of the University. The story I am about to tell occurred a few years ago at the Society of Mining Engineers banquet, which is held in the spring of the year. Earl had sold his antimony mine at Stampede to this big company, with the understanding that they were going to mine the ore. Well the night of the banquet the executive director, I think it was, announced that the company was going to donate that mine to the University of Alaska Fairbanks. Earl at that time was in his 80s and recognized immediately that the purchase of his mine was nothing more that a write-off by the big company. The announcement infuriated Earl. To calm him down I was asked to go dance with Earl, which I did. We were out on the dance floor, and wouldn't you know it, this executive decided he wanted to dance with his wife, so they entered the dance floor. Well, Earl was still boiling and as we danced around the floor he maneuvered us over next to this guy, and when we got close Earl took a poke at him. Fortunately he missed and the guy left the dance floor. I think this did Earl a lot of good, because he simmered down, and we finished that dance and a couple more. The evening went smoothly after that.

Jim: That is a great first-hand story about one of Alaska's most colorful and rugged pioneers, Leah. By the way how big was that executive?

Leah: Compared to Earl he was a giant, and of course he was much younger.

Jim: I am looking forward to getting together with you and Jim Lounsbury to write Earl Pilgrim's story. Leah, thank you for joining us today here on Alaska Gold Trails.

Leah: It was a pleasure to be here, Jim. I've enjoyed the interview.

The Life of
Earl Pilgrim
(1896-1987)

Photograph courtesy of Jim Lounsbury

Earl Pilgrim
with
Jim Lounsbury and Leah Madonna
October 1985

Leah: Thank you for giving this interview, Earl, and thank you for helping out, Jim. One of these days we hope to publish a few of these interviews as a tribute to those healthy pioneers of the early 20th century that opened up this country. How are you?

Earl: Oh I'm healthy, but I don't consider myself a pioneer like many of those guys. I came in here late in the deal.

Leah: How do you stay so healthy, Earl, and where were you born? Give us a little of your background.

Earl: I was born in Durango, Colorado, in 1896. Let me start with my parents. My father was born on a farm in Iowa. At the age of 11 he started smoking. At the same time he says, "There's enough people on the farm to support the family and run the farm." He climbed on the railroad going west. He got to the end, where they were extending it. They needed help on the construction, so they put him to work right away as a teamster on a scraper. Back then they didn't have no child labor laws. That was probably five or six years after the Civil War had ended, because he remembers being a small boy in a country school during the Civil War, when two men came to arrest two big kids who were in the same school, for failure to show up for the draft, and they also took a prisoner. They had to take them through the woods. The two guards were killed, and these two boys escaped. So they had draft evasion in the Civil War in Iowa. Anyway, Dad worked on the construction of the transcontinental railroad several years. Then he went home, and he told everyone all about the glories of the West, the game on the prairies, and all that. He took his brother with him when he went back. They traveled and hunted buffalo for the railroads. I think my dad was more adventurous and rugged than I ever was. One day he rode into Durango, Colorado, on horseback. My mother, a young lady, arrived with her family in a covered wagon. My dad married her. I don't know why she liked him. Maybe she liked him because he had three fingers missing on his right hand. He was working in the smelter at that time and he had to switch the ore cars that came into the smelter. They would unhook them from the train or hook them up. Either way they used the old coupling pin, which was just a loose pin. He had a pin in the eye, holding it in one end or branch of the train, and he would hold it up. When the train brought the car in he would drop the pin down and couple them up. One time something went wrong—the train came in too fast or something—and it smashed three fingers off his right hand.

Leah: How long did he live?

Earl: At 98, he had a prostate operation; otherwise he would have lived to be over 100. My father was probably as serious as a toothache that had to be extracted. He went home and he demanded his clothes. We argued with him, but he was a stubborn old guy, so we gave him his clothes. He took a spade and started spading up the garden. He started to hemorrhage internally and went into the living room, sat down and died. Mother was putting up the washing in the rear of the house, and Dad was gone. Anyway, if I'm as good as he is at 98, I'll be real proud of myself. Keep up the family records.

Leah: And how old are you today?

Earl: I'm 89, but my good health isn't my fault; it was because of my ancestors. My dad was a true Westerner. It was remarkable how he could have done all those things and gone through all that time without getting a disease. Most of those early men pioneers in the western towns went to town sometimes. But one thing, those women of ill-repute kept good care of their health, and their venereal disease wasn't as prevalent as it is now. I remember once in college the coach, Doc Hall, gave us a lecture—every year he gave it to his track team. He said, "If you guys feel that you gotta have a piece of tail," "why" he said, "Go get a professional woman who does that for a living, not some floozy who is handing it out. Those professional women have to take care of themselves—that's their business." Maybe that's what kept my father healthy in his early days.

Jim: How old was your grandfather when he died?

Earl: My grandfather was killed on the farm. Doesn't count.

Jim: Excuse me, your great-grandfather.

Earl: No, he doesn't count either. You mean my great-great grandfather?

Jim: Yeah, your great-great grandfather, he was...

Earl: A hundred and eight.

Leah: Oh my!

Jim: A hundred and eight, can you imagine that?

Earl: It's on his tombstone up in Indiana.

Leah: When did you first start mining, Earl?

Earl: I started out when I was just five years old. My father was into mining and my mother's brothers were miners. They were coal miners. They found this coal seam nearby, and in those days you could stake coal just like mining claims. I don't think I was over five years old. Anyway, this uncle was foreman of this Ute Coal. Ute's an Indian name from the Paiute Indians. I remember, I could give the Paiute war hoot when I was a little kid just as good as any chief or any Indian warrior. To be honest, I really started working in mines while I was attending college.

Leah: When did you first come to Alaska?

Earl: I first came to Alaska to work in the Treadwell Mines in the summer of 1915 while I was going to college. There were four mines: the Treadwell, Mexican, Ready Bullion and I forget the other one. There was a barren spot between the Treadwell and the Ready Bullion. Other than that the vein was mineable low-grade ore for about two miles. I mean, the vein was continuous—it wasn't faulted in all that distance. It was a big vein, over 100 feet wide. From the Ready Bullion they drove a tunnel through to connect it to the other mines. They had concrete walls to dam it and a waterproof door so that if the Ready Bullion got flooded by the ocean they could still work the other mines.

Leah: Did they ever need to dam it?

Earl: Oh yeah, but it happened the other way. The Treadwell broke and the ocean came in. The Ready Bullion worked several years after that.

Jim: Were you working in the Treadwell mine when it flooded?

Earl: Yes. I was brand-new to that mine. We were down working at the 770-foot level. That was about 700 feet below sea level. I thought it was the ocean coming in and so did everyone else. I was in the ore-transfer station with an Italian man, and he didn't know any more than I did. Although, come to think of it, I had been there working longer. A lot of men worked a few days to get a grubstake, then left. The teamster drove a team and hauled two cars of ore from back in the drift. The horses or mules were trained to come fast on a trot, and when they arrived in the station they turned off, and the car ran off and over the chute, and we had to stand over the rails, which were about ten inches apart, and rake the big chunks of ore so they would pass through the grizzly and into the chute. From there the ore was drawn into buckets and hoisted to the surface. I was just one little newcomer there. I was doing this on summer vacation. I got away from the flood. All of us on that level got out of there without getting hurt. Others weren't so lucky.

Leah: This was in the summer of 1915?

Earl: Yes. I was getting $60 a month.

Jim: Earl was quite an athlete back then. He won a month's wages in one day, on the Fourth of July. Tell Leah how that happened, Earl.

Earl: I shouldn't have done that because that made me a professional. I was on the University of Washington track team and I thought the mining company's foot race was amateur. When I won that race the judges yelled at me to come over. I thought they were going to give me a medal or pin or something, but they handed me $50 in gold coins. It was so much, I accepted it. Thinking it over, I should have given it back. It cost me my amateur standing.

Jim: Leah, he once told me the whole story about when he was running that foot race. Remember, it was the beginning of the First World War. There was a guy that was racing against him named Dermany, and he thought that they were yelling, "Come on, Germany!" when they were yelling "Come on Dermany!" and Earl took off like a wild man. Just before he got to the finish line some guy says, "Take her easy lad, you're a mile ahead of 'em." Tell Leah the story, Earl.

Earl: Oh yes, this fellow Dermont. I'd see these fellows running around there training. You could tell they were running for track or something, and I asked somebody and they said well that's a two-mile foot race on the Fourth of July. I had been on the University of Washington track team the spring before and I figured I would enter that race, but I didn't need to do any training; I'm getting enough exercise hammering and picking down underground. So, on the Fourth of July, I put on a track suit and a pair of tennis shoes and lined up. I got a picture of the runners when they lined up. I was on the inside of the track. When they fired the pistol, I took off, and here come four runners past me, and I thought boy they're pretty fast, faster than I am for a two-mile race, but I kept track of them. I passed one of them, I passed another one, pretty soon they were all behind me, nobody ahead of me. People kept yelling, "Come on Germany!" I guess I had Germany on the mind because of the war. I kept thinking he was right on my tail, but I'd been trained in college when you wear track shoes, you never look over you shoulder, you'll stumble and hurt yourself. Finally, now this was on Douglas Island in Alaska, some old guy yelled, "Take'er easy lad. You're a mile ahead of 'em." I've used it as my criteria ever since.

Jim: Who was the gentleman who told you last summer his dad was superintendent of the mine, and when he was just a young kid watched you win that road race.

Earl: His dad was the general manager of all the Treadwell mines.

Jim: This "kid" is a retired gentleman now, and he phoned Earl last summer and talked to him for a half an hour from California and said, "You were my idol when I was just a kid in Juneau." That was pretty nice of him.

Earl: Well I wasn't there very long to be an idol. I was just there a little over four months.

Jim: Well, Earl is being too modest, Leah. He also won the first aid contest, on his crew.

Earl: Jim remembers everything better than I do, and he wasn't even born yet.

Leah: What did you do after you graduated from college?

Earl: I worked in different mines. I graduated from the College of Mines, University of Washington, in 1916. As I said, every summer vacation I was mining, and after I left college I went to work in the Coeur d'Alene Mining District. It was the Upper Bunker Hill Mine.

Jim: Were you a surveyor in that mine?

Earl: Yes, I was a young engineer for the mine. The mine has to have an engineer to make certain the tunnels are driven in the right direction.

Jim: That was an inclined shaft you were working there. I saw that picture. You had your transit, getting ready to go underground.

Earl: Yes, that was a pretty good-sized mine, a medium-sized mine. They had a ten-mile standard-gauge railroad connected with the regular standard railroads, so the ores could be hauled directly on the standard cars.

Leah: Where did you go after that mine?

Earl: I get mixed up on which way I went.

Jim: Before the war you were in Canada. Tell us that little story.

Earl: Before I graduated and after graduation are all mixed up, but anyway I was pursuing the same mining work. I accepted this job near Vancouver, B.C. Not very far from Lake Kootenay. Beautiful lake, most beautiful mining camp I ever was in. The lake was 80-odd miles long and we were right down on the shore. The snow falls early and I had to get out of my house, which was my engineering residence and office. I had to go out twice and shovel the snow away from the chimney on my roof. That was before November. The snow was so deep that when they hauled me and my trunk down to the lake the horses were wearing snowshoes. Did you ever see snowshoes on a horse?

Leah: No, not on a horse.

Earl: Well, the horses knew how to wear them on their four feet and they're perfectly round, strapped onto the bottom of the hooves.

Jim: Tell Leah about the fellow that introduced you to your wife, and your time in W.W.I.

Earl: The man who took me with him to the party where I met her was Clyde Pangborne who was a civil engineer on construction of the Bunker Hill Smelter. When the war came on I didn't see him anymore. What he had done was become a pilot. After the war he flew the first plane from Tokyo to Wenatchee. He had flown over to Tokyo to collect his $50,000 prize for the first plane to fly the Pacific. When he arrived there and he wasn't a Japanese flyer the newspaper in Tokyo canceled that $50,000. Since that $50,000 was not available, he got his plane all ready, and he took off, and since his mother lived in Wenatchee he flew on over, past Seattle, and landed in Wenatchee.

Leah: What caused you to enter the war?

Earl: When the United States had just gone to war, I read about this regiment. The 27th Engineers was recruiting miners to drive tunnels under the Austrian Alps. These Alps were highly fortified, and the Allies couldn't get to them. There weren't any airplanes to drop bombs. In a narrow place, the artillery didn't do much damage. They wanted this pass, but it was kind of a stalemate. The United States wasn't in it yet. Everybody was praying and hoping we would get in it, and pour our hundreds of thousands of troops in, and push Kaiser Bill back into Germany. So this regiment that had been picked by the Joint Chiefs of Staff was American miners with American equipment to drive adits or tunnels underneath the Alps and blast the enemy all to hell. That was what this regiment was to do. They started recruiting for that, I believe, before we had officially entered the war. Men volunteered for that. The *Engineering and Mining Journal* notarized it so much that miners were coming to enlist from every mining camp in the United States, especially in the West. It was a very interesting outfit to be with, because there would be groups in the barracks or anywhere, and surprisingly not talking about girls all the time, but talking about this mine in Bisbee, Arizona, or that one in Coeur d'Alene, Idaho, or mining education itself. It was just interesting talking with roughneck miners or young engineers. I figured probably a third of that 1,500 men were young engineers like me, who had enlisted as privates. Another third were older engineers who had resigned from jobs—halfway important jobs. Up until recently I have seen names in the *Engineering and Mining Journal* of some manager at some mine, who had served in that regiment. The other third were just roughneck miners, but they all knew mining and could talk about mining.

Leah: You were talking about flying a little bit ago. Did you know or ever fly with Ben Eielson?

Earl: Oh yes. When I think of Ben and his little airplane it reminds me of my first airplane ride. World War I—that's where I had my first ride in an airplane, was at the tail end of W.W.I. We had been shipped back to the United States. I had been transferred to the 217th Engineers and was a lieutenant. We were shipped back after the war to a military base in Louisiana, and we were waiting to be discharged, and there was some planes flying—some little planes—two or three miles away. We were just waiting around with nothing to do, so one day I asked the stable sergeant for a horse, and I rode over there to take a look. I saw a lieutenant—same rating as me—and an engineer. We shook hands and I asked him what he was doing with this group of pilots. They had a different insignia. It was a branch of the Army. He said they were experimenting by trying to install radios to make ground-to-air communications. They had never done that in W.W.I. He was an electrical engineer with the same insignia as an engineer. I told him that I sure would like to ride in one of those things. He said, "I think I can arrange it." He asked me where my outfit was stationed. I pointed and said, "Over there. You can get me on the phone at the 217th Engineers." One morning he called up and said, "Come over tomorrow and you can go up." So I arranged with the stable sergeant for a horse. Of course in those war days we were just like everybody nowadays—they won't walk half a block, they got to ride. In any case I had to ride a horse. You didn't hear me say that.

Jim: That's all right. I ride a horse too.

Earl: So anyway, I galloped over there and the lieutenant was there and he said, "Well those pilots are not out yet. They go to town every night and get drunk." They had these little planes, a bunch of them I guess, just about like the "Jenny" out at the airport. No brakes on them. The engine turned the propeller over real slow, and a wedge of wood was placed against each wheel to hold it. By and by a bunch of motorcycles arrived with sidecars, and in each pocket was a drunk lieutenant. The Lieutenant introduced me to the pilot that was going to fly this plane—the plane they used for testing radio communication. This was my first flight, and we took off on that dirt field. He tipped the plane one way and that was fun and then he tipped it the other way and that was fun too. Then we got up maybe 4,000 feet and he yelled something and he started to do a loop—that's what I thought—and he got it up almost over and there we were, we didn't go any farther, and then she come down spinning around right toward the airstrip and I thought this was it, and finally he got her straightened out and it came right out. Then he flew her around a little; then he landed it. After I got out of the plane he said, "That's the way we sober up every morning." That was my first flight. That was just before I was discharged in 1918. Six years later I met Ben.

Jim: After you got out of the service is when you went to Nevada, is that right?

Earl: Yes, I worked in Goodsprings, Nevada, in a zinc mine, for Mr. Kirk, as his engineer. I respected him a great deal. The mine and smelter was taken over by National Lead, which was one of the big mining companies and manufacturers. They manufacture all sorts of things. Anyway, Mr. Kirk was in charge of this smelter, and I was made superintendent of the smelter, or manager, or whatever the title was.

Leah: What made you leave a good job like that and come to Fairbanks?

Earl: One day I received a letter from the University of Washington College of Mines. The department head had recommended me for the job of Professor of Mining Engineering and Metallurgy at the new college starting in Fairbanks, Alaska. I accepted the job and I guess that it was probably the biggest mistake I ever made, coming up here to this stinking little college.

Leah: How many buildings were at the college when you arrived?

Earl: There was only one building here when I arrived. I didn't know that when I started the trip north.

Leah: I have read about your teaching at the University when it was the School of Mines. I imagine it was pretty interesting when it was just one old building. When you came, Earl, had the school already started or was it the beginning?

Earl: It was the beginning. The school had not been started yet. I was the first. There were five of us, I think. You know, I was just sick—not ill, but disappointed, when I arrived. I had envisioned buildings and all that. When I met and learned to know Judge Bunnell that made it worse. He lived solely to build up his record and compare it to the man that defeated him in election for Alaska delegate. Right from the start I figured Judge Bunnell was an ex-politician and a windbag—a first class windbag—and I never changed my mind on that. He had run for delegate for Congress. We were a territory then. The only representative we had in the U.S. Congress was a delegate, and Wickersham was a famous pioneer and he had been the delegate to Congress several times and was well-known all over Alaska and had done a great many things. And Bunnell had been a federal judge. I think at that time, I don't know for sure, but federal judges in Alaska were appointed by the president of the United States. I believe that is the way it was done, but I am not positive. Anyway, the time I made up my mind about Bunnell was when I first arrived. My wife and I went to dinner with Bunnell and his wife at their home. All this guy did at their home that evening was criticize Mrs. Bunnell's cooking, and she was a nice woman and a fine motherly woman. That's when I arrived at the conclusion that the president of the college was a windbag and nothing else, and I learned that he had run for election in politics against Wickersham and he was defeated and he didn't have a job, so some of the political people in Alaska promoted him to be the first president of the college. It wasn't because of his superior knowledge and education. I always considered him a windbag, and I never changed my mind on that subject.

Jim: Maybe if you tell us a little something about the first tennis court at the University of Alaska that would help us understand your feelings toward Bunnell. You were involved in trying to get it started, weren't you?

Earl: I suggested it. My brother, the druggist, and Root Tilford. Root drove a wagon for some kind of clean-up service, women's clothes or something like that. He was a wiry little footracer. He was always running races on Sunday at the parks for money. He could run the 100-yards very fast. He was purely a professional runner, not an amateur. This group of us—the druggist, my brother, Root Tilford and I—built the first tennis court, a dirt bottom. It wasn't any work just leveling it off, padding it down, rolling it a little bit. We all played tennis there, and I became a pretty good tennis player. I wanted to start a tennis court out at the college. I suggested it to Bunnell. He said, "Oh no, you couldn't have anything like that. It's too noisy and it would be right close here to the building." It was the very next year that he put a notice on the bulletin board that they were building a tennis court.

Jim: Earl was the highest paid professor up there.

Earl: That's true, I got $50 a year more than any of the others—$1,550 a year. Truesdale was professor of civil engineering. He is still alive. We went and visited him where he lives down in Seattle.

Jim: Who was the guy we visited down on Third Avenue that was one of the professors up there?

Earl: That was Bob Brown. He was a fraternity brother but I don't think he was a member of the original fraternity. I was professor of Mining Engineering and Metallurgy, but the main object of the school was to promote agriculture and mining, so they had the professor of agriculture, and being a typical farmer he arrived with a wife and two or three children.

Leah: Was it hard to find a place to live when you got up here? Fairbanks was pretty small at that time.

Earl: Small, yes. We lived down below the campus hill, but I can't remember exactly where anymore.

Jim: They ran that narrow-gauge train two or three times a day to the University, didn't they?

Earl: They had a locomotive hooked onto one coach. Very often it was nothing but the caboose. So I generally walked or trotted up, all winter long. My wife came up with me. She was very well educated but she didn't have very good health. Her father owned a mine in the Coeur' d' Alene'-Bunker Hill upper workings. They had sent her to the best doctors, but she still didn't have good health.

Jim: That is when you and Ben Eielson became good buddies isn't it?

Earl: Oh yes. We arrived about the same time in Fairbanks. Ben taught history at the high school and of course I taught at the University. We both coached basketball teams and we played against each other. We didn't have a gym at the University so we played in an old skating rink on Third or Fourth Avenue, and it had a good floor, and it wasn't in use, so Ben got up a basketball team at the high school, and I got one up at the University. I gathered up what few boys we had and made a basketball team out of them. Three pretty-good-sized brothers—the Loftus boys— they were the guards and center of the team. Judge Bunnell was there when we played basketball against the high school teachers and students. The high school had Ben Eielson, a fine forward. That was the first game the college had played against anybody. At the end of the first half they were 20 points ahead of us. I went over to Bunnell. "How about me guarding Ben?" He looked at me, then in his most dignified expression at the ceiling. In due time he said, "They're playing their coach (Ben), so I guess it's alright for you to play." It was at the old Armory. So I guarded Ben. I controlled him, but they still beat us by two points in the varsity game.

Jim: Shaved'er by 18 points. That's pretty good for one half. I'd say you did a pretty good job of keeping the score down.

Earl: Ben and I were very very good friends. When my wife and I heard he was gone, we both cried.

Jim: We were out at the airport two days ago and saw his airplane. What did they call that airplane?

Earl: The Jenny.

Jim: The Jenny, yeah. They had it hanging up inside the airport terminal on display.

Earl: Ben was working for small pay. He was probably getting less pay than I was. He got some businessmen in town to put up some money to buy that surplused Jenny. I think $2,500 or maybe less is what he paid.

Leah: Did you fly with any other famous pilots, like maybe Gillam?

Earl: Oh I have flown with Harold many times.

Jim: Believe it or not Leah, he has a movie picture of Harold.

Earl: Did you say that Harold is still here?

Jim: No. Harold's son, Harold Jr. is still here, but Harold Sr. is no longer alive.

Earl: He was about my age. Maybe younger.

Leah: Was Earl Beistline a student of yours?

Earl: No he came later. But, he was a student in the school here. My wife, who now lives on the 15th floor of a retirement home in Portland, Oregon, told me just a few days ago that she knew him from the schools in Juneau. His home was there. I never knew him, not while I was connected with the college. I met him later; quite a few years later, for the first time.

Jim: He just got some kind of honorary award. He's been at the University for quite a few years now.

Earl: You know, Earl told me he wanted to give me some great honor, I don't know what. I says, "The only honor I want here is my letter for playing basketball on the University of Alaska basketball team."

Jim: They gave it to him too, they gave him a letter and jacket and the whole nine yards.

Leah: Harold Jr. just took one of Jim's prospecting classes.

Earl: What about Harold and Jim now?

Leah: My husband, Jim, teaches the University of Alaska short courses in prospecting and Harold just recently completed one of those courses. I think it was Geochemical Prospecting. When you were teaching at the School of Mines in Fairbanks, did you teach any of the short courses for the miners and the prospectors.

Earl: Oh yes, we had those. I know your husband, Jim, teaches several courses similar to some that I taught. In fact a bunch of my courses were short courses. The students liked them because I had knocked around the mines so much. I could present the information how it really was done as well as the theory.

Jim: The students really like it when the teacher can back up the theory with experience. I have taken some of Jim's courses and he does that extremely well.

Earl: That was young Harold, Jim taught. It was old Harold that flew me all over. He flew me to Nebesna quite a few times—to the Nebesna Mine. After I left the University the mining companies would hire me to go to the mines in various parts of Alaska to advise them on mining, as a consultant.

Leah: Did you ever get down to the Hatcher Pass area around the Lucky Shot and Independence mines?

Earl: Yes I was there once. I didn't spend much time getting acquainted with that country.

Leah: They were hard rock mining there in the late 30s and early 40s. It was W.W.II that shut down their operation, plus it was faulted and they lost the vein.

Earl: I heard they were having problems there.

Leah: Why did you leave the University?

Earl: It was getting uncomfortable there, and I wanted to go mining. Bunnell and I didn't exactly get along. I don't think he liked me any better than I liked him. I remember when I was leaving the place, I dropped into his office. I made some remark which I knew would get him mad. He said, "Bullshit!" I said, "Bullshit? You're the biggest bullshitter in all Alaska." He started to tremble, and I said, "Go ahead." He was shaking all over and his face turned purple. I figured he was going to have a stroke. I said, "Go ahead and have a stroke. I've seen quite a few men die and it won't break my heart at all." I walked out the door.

Jim: What year was it that you left the University?

Earl: It was 1928. I worked there four years.

Leah: Let's change direction here. I understand you were good friends with Eva McGown?

Earl: Yes, I knew her well.

Leah: I met Eva many years ago.

Earl: What happened to Eva?

Leah: She died in the Nordale Hotel fire.

Jim: You know the interesting thing about that...a week before she died I was in the Nordale Hotel and when I talked to her—she talks to everybody—she was going to her room on the second floor, and she told me that she had just moved from the first to the second floor, and so I opened the elevator door for her, pushed the button and ran the elevator up to the second floor then I went back down. That was the last time I ever saw her. She was explaining to me how she had just recently moved to the "penthouse" upstairs she called it. I was down working in the coal mines in Healy when I turned the TV on and learned the Nordale Hotel was on fire.

Earl: Everybody knew her and liked her.

Leah: All the miners used to come into town when I first got here, and they would all go see Eva.

Earl: She was a central part of the community.

Leah: Some, from what I have been told, would even leave their gold with her for safekeeping.

Earl: Yes, I remember that; they did. She was well respected and trusted. Eva was older than me of course; probably closer to Jim's father's age.

Jim: Leah, speaking of people that Earl knew, have you ever heard about Fanny Quigly? The Fanny Quigly that had the Red Top Mine?

Leah: No.

Jim: They were friends of Earl's. That was a colorful couple there. She traveled with a kicker sled, from the Klondike to Nome, without any dogs or anything, by herself. So anyhow, Earl can tell you a story about this, and I'll let him tell it. All the old-timers like Earl knew Fanny Quigly.

Earl: Oh, I'd better not tell it. Besides, I never figured I was an "old-timer."

Jim: What was the first mining you did in Alaska after you left the University?

Earl: I was placer mining out on Happy Creek.

Jim: How long did you mine at Happy Creek?

Earl: I was there two-and-a-half years.

Jim: You were telling me one time about Nome Creek. You had ground staked at Nome Creek about that same time. You sold it for a cigar at the Nordale Hotel or something?

Earl: Yeah, an Optimo Cigar—a two-bit cigar. I traded the whole works off for a two-bit cigar. Funny, I still remember his name—Cliff McCall. He had taken over Nome Creek later.

Jim: Is that when you ran into the Swedes—Coat and Vest? On that trip?

Earl: Yes. Two partners, they were always together in town—every bar, everywhere, and the old-timers called them Coat and Vest.

Jim: It didn't dawn on me who Coat and Vest were until he got to telling me about these two guys. Come to find out they built the house that he owns and lives in now.

Earl: One of these days I'm going to write my life story.

Jim: You're not ready to write your memoirs yet because you're still making history.

Leah: You'll probably be out there mining this next summer, won't you, Earl?

Earl: Yeah, mining is the only fun there is. Your age doesn't matter if you got good health.

Jim: And did you go to the Newsboy from Happy Creek?

Earl: No, just before I left there an Irishman—an old-timer by the name of Jack Donnelly—asked me if he could live in that cabin down there. He thought I had it. I said, "I don't own that cabin, but I'll find out." Whoever I found said it was just a vacant, clean, little cabin open to anyone who wanted to live in it. Jack was our cook, and he didn't want to live in town. He preferred to live out there. So he moved into the cabin. Then he asked me who owned that land. I said, "I don't know. It's open for location, I guess." He says, "I'd like to sink a shaft there. How deep do you think it is to bedrock?" I said, "Off-hand, I couldn't tell you. The land's sloping up, so maybe 25—30 feet." So he borrowed a windless from me. When he got down so far, working by himself, climbing up his ladder, and then hoisting the bucket up, it was deeper than that. So he went to town and got a friend to work with him. Finally Jack came up and said, "Earl, there's nothing down there but old quartz boulders on the bedrock." My ears perked up. I said, "Quartz?" Later I went down with a dog team and sled to get the windless, and there was some quartz on the surface that he'd brought up, and it was vein quartz. I noticed there was gas coming out of the shaft. So much gas, in fact, that there was not enough oxygen for candles to burn. It would put them out. So I didn't go down the shaft then, but I threw this quartz on the sled. And I was in a hurry so I dumped the windless and threw several pieces of that quartz on the ground right in front of the bunkhouse. In the spring, I put a couple of men to work at the Happy Creek Mine. They were living in the bunkhouse. When I stopped at the bunkhouse to say something, I pointed to that quartz lying there and said, "Jack found a vein down there, someplace." I assumed Jack had hit the vein, but he didn't know anything about quartz veins. One of those men standing there looked down at that quartz and said, "That's good ore." He could see golden specks all over a piece that weighed about ten pounds. And I looked at it and it sure was good gold ore.

Leah: Did that discovery become a mine?

Earl: Yes, it's known as the Grant Mine.

Leah: Tell us what you did then.

Earl: Well, I went over, and Jack was cooking for Joe Henderson. Joe Henderson was mining right up close to a quartz vein there. So I stopped there and said, "Jack, you'd better go over and stake that. That's a rich gold vein." "I don't want it," he said real fast. "I don't want anything to do with it." Well I stood there about five minutes trying to convince him, but he refused to stake it.

Jim: Was Jack a placer miner?

Earl: Yeah.

Jim: Most placer miners don't want anything to do with lode. They would just as soon stay away from it.

Earl: I said, "Well you don't object if I stake it?" "No, go ahead," he said. So I went out and I put two claims in. The Irishman #1 and the Irishman #2, after Jack, and used the shaft for the discovery.

Jim: Oh I see. So Jack originally sunk the shaft for placer.

Earl: Yeah, he was just curious that's all. He wanted to kill time, get exercise. So then, that fall, that shaft laid there open all summer and it slumped in a great deal, and I got O.M. Grant to go in with me. I knew him from over in the Kantishna.

Jim: Did you hire him or was he a partner?

Earl: Oh, we just went in as partners. When I put my stakes on the claims, I told Grant to put his name on the location, so he was a partner. Then that fall we cleaned that shaft out. There was all that quartz lying in the bottom of the shaft. Now what direction to find the vein. Well I thought it sloped from Ester Dome downward, so I told him to start cross-drifting on bedrock. The first day we hoisted nothing but vein quartz. The next day, not so much, and so on. Pretty soon, he was sending up no vein quartz, and he wanted to quit. So I said, "Well, let me down and take over." I went down, and I could see then that we were not drifting uphill. We were going a little downhill. There was kind of a swell in the bedrock. So I says, "We'll go the other way." Grant says, "The hell with that. Were wasting time on this." I said, "If we don't get that within a week, or two or three days, I'll pay you time for it." We went the opposite way about 10 or 12 feet and there was a nice little vein of gold-bearing quartz. That became the Grant Mine.

Leah: What happened next. What did you do next?

Earl: It would have taken a lot of work to re-timber that old shaft, so we sank a new shaft right alongside of it. Probably, if you go out there now, you could find evidence of the old shaft.

Jim: The last time I was out there they were using the old Irishman shaft for a settling pond.

Earl: The first shaft that the Irishman sank—the same one we used to discover the hard rock lode—was just a few feet from the vein. In the morning, especially when the barometric pressure had dropped, there'd be gas coming out, so I'd go to the opening and build a fire in this stove, and I had pipe running clear down to the bottom, about 100 feet. Using the rising heat we could suck the gas that had accumulated up and out of the shaft. Some days it was so gassy we would have to keep burning the stove and put on a suction pump. One morning, I'd gone down there an hour or two earlier than the other two boys; Grant and Pete Nikov were working underground, and I was working on the hoist. I had pumped the shaft out and I had lowered the candle to the bottom, and it burned on the bottom, but just as I set it down, it landed on top of a little rock or something and tipped over. Grant crawled down first, but he was a "big-time-miner" then—he owned a half interest in a hard rock gold mine. I noticed he was more bossy, and more big shot, but he was a good worker. Anyway, that morning he crawled down, and he called up through the pipe and he says, "Whaddya mean? You trying to kill me sending me down here in all this gas?" And I yelled down, "If there is gas down there, don't just stand there, climb on out!" He came up yelling that I was trying to kill him by sending him down. I figured he got too much of that arrogance. A day or so later I said, "I'm leaving. I'm walking away from here." So that's what I did. I never had anything more to do with him. We had been working in Joe Henderson's mill. I had gotten permission from Joe. We were treating our ore there and he hired a man—I won't mention his name because his family may be around here—he had worked for the Cleary Hill off and on for a number of years—he knew all about underground mining and he knew all about saving gold and melting it, and Grant had him working for him. One day when I came in from Stampede, Mrs. Nordale told me that in this man's home, a plumber went down in the basement to do some repairs and found three bars of gold cached there.

Jim: The guy that was working for Grant? The guy that was treating the ore?

Earl: Yeah, the guy that was treating their ore. He had also worked for the Cleary Hill Mine, the richest gold mine in the Cleary Creek area. He had somehow accumulated a few gold bars between Cleary and Joe Henderson's ground. If I had known that when the news went around town, I would have borrowed a gun and taken one or two of those bars. But by that time he had undoubtedly moved them to some other location.

Jim: Leah, Earl claims he doesn't have an enemy in the world—he outlived them all.

Earl: That's what you say. I didn't say that.

Jim: I guess I did. You're right.

Leah: Where did you go after you left the Grant Mine, Earl?

Earl: I went to the Newsboy. It was 1931. I worked there until 1936 or maybe '37.

Leah: Where was the Newsboy?

Earl: Out here on Cleary Summit. When gold was struck in Fairbanks I guess they began prospecting every creek. A fellow by the name of Hersburger found the Newsboy vein in 1911. It was a little larger vein than the Cleary Hill, which was one of the richest veins. The Newsboy had good ore but it wasn't quite as rich as the Cleary Hill. But it was a little larger vein, and a bunch of people who were very inexperienced at mining a gold vein, or any kind of vein for that matter, were running it, and they built a mill on the surface right close to the collar of the shaft they sunk 360 feet deep, and they found water in the shaft. I guess they figured that water would be enough to run the mill. They sold stock in the Newsboy, locally, to raise money. The newspaper said it was going to be a big mine and all this and that.

Jim: In Fairbanks in 1911, they sold 100,000 shares in 24 hours didn't they Earl?

Earl: Yeah, but they ran out of water and that closed them down. The water in the mine wasn't near enough to run the mill. They had a five-stamp mill, which was a good little gold saver in those days and it is today. There are several of them working in California and other places. So they tore the mill building down and that took a lot of labor. They moved it down the hill into Cleary Creek on a piece of land there and were milling the ore. Horse-drawn wagons would come down and then go up an incline above the crusher and ore bin and dump the ore. That was there when I arrived in 1931. It was old and in rickety shape, but I hauled enough ore down to fill the ore bin, and I got it all ready to start. We found the boiler leaked. It had a water boiler underneath the firebox. Some of those boilers had a slim space about eight inches wide—too slim to crawl into to work on. That was underneath the firebox, and when we filled it with water, that leaked. We pulled that boiler out and put another one in. We had to take the side of the building out to remove the first one and put the other one in. The day we closed up the side and had this new boiler full of water and a fire in the firebox, we must have laid the hot ashes too close to the side of the building, and that night those ashes must have started a fire. That is the only explanation I could come up with. At first I thought somebody that disliked me had set fire to the building. There was a placer miner that lived down there about 200 yards from the mill. I think his name was Tom King. At first I thought he might have set fire to the mill. Then I figured, no, he wouldn't do a thing like that. Somebody had come over and shot his revolver on the lock on the mill and tried to get in and put out the fire. For certain, someone saw the fire. Anyway I didn't ask them about it. Everyone around there knew it had burned clear down with the bin full of ore. I guess that's still lying there. I hadn't found the rich vein. I continued to work at the Newsboy trying to find that vein. Everything had been disappointing, and I walked away from it, but I kept it in mind over these past 42 or 43 years.

Jim: Well we have plenty of time to fool around with it. It would be a nice little retirement thing for you. Who knows? That mother lode may still be there waiting for you. Leah, for his 89th birthday I went up and prospected it for him. I found the fault, and all we have to do now is run some geophysical tests on it and see where it goes. A fellow is going to come out in the next couple of weeks and run those tests for us. If the results are good, Earl will be a wealthy miner before too long. What do you think of that, Earl?

Earl: That would be nice. Then I could go mining in a half dozen other places. As far as I am concerned mining is the only fun in the world that I can think of.

Jim: Somewhere around the time you left the Newsboy didn't you have a coal option on a lease or something down by Usibelli.

Earl: Oh yes, I had plans. That was right after the Newsboy in 1931. I had an option with the owners of a big plant to supply coal, but I didn't have any money to put up for equipment to transport it to this business in Fairbanks. I can't seem to remember their name. Anyway, we had to ship it in and leave it on the banks of the Chena River until spring. I asked them to postpone the deal completely until spring and I could get it over across the river, but they wouldn't do it, so I never went ahead with the project. Probably some day it would've made money.

Jim: Leah, after Earl left that coal deal he put in 40-some-odd years over at Stampede; he has about three miles of underground tunnel work. You just wouldn't believe how much work he has done over there.

Leah: What year did you go to Stampede, Earl?

Earl: I went into Stampede in 1938, right after my little coal adventure.

Leah: Is it over there that you had the bear and the martin?

Jim: Tell her about the black bear, Mrs. Black, Earl.

Earl: Every now and then Mrs. Black Bear would drop in on me at night. She liked the dark nights. She came around from the time she was a young lady until she was up quite large the last time. One night I had moved my bed into the kitchen because there were so many animals. Any night, almost, I could expect to have an animal outside trying to get into the screen box where we kept our meat and perishables. One night I looked out at the commotion and Mrs. Black had hold of some meat. She had unlatched the cooler and relatched it. That explained the disappearing meat mystery. Later I fooled her; I put a Frigidaire in the mess house. For years I had been thinking of how I could get a windmill high enough to run a generator to provide just enough power to run the Frigidaire and a few things, so I could have electric lights to read by. Something we could use in the wintertime for the bunkhouse at Stampede. At first it was nip and tuck, until we built up the mine. It became the second largest producer of antimony in the United States. I had to build an airfield so I could quit hauling my ore by sled to the railroad during January, February and March. With an airfield I could fly over any time of year and haul out the ore. That was almost finished when this man named Dole talked me into selling the mine.

Jim: That was the largest privately owned airfield in Alaska. Isn't it almost 5,000 feet long?

Earl: It wasn't quite finished. I was going to make it 5,000 feet long. Now it is only about 4,300 feet.

Jim: How much ore could the mill process in a day?

Earl: Well it would handle about 20 tons every 24 hours. Not very big by today's standards.

Leah: How many years were you over there?

Earl: Almost exactly 40 years. People said that I could never get a ton of ore to the railroad. And it looked like they were right, but I finally got the National Lead Company to back me, I think more to get me off their back. They told me they would grubstake me to go ahead and try and get 300 tons of crude ore. They had visited the mine and it was good high grade ore. I had taken them in with an eight-horse pack train. They said, "This was a beautiful trip and we enjoyed it very much, (it was right through Mt. McKinley Park) but you can't get any ore out of here." "Well," I said, "I could." I told them how, but they didn't believe me. Finally in the Nordale Hotel later they said, "We still don't believe you can do it, but we'll grubstake you." That showed they had some faith in me. That was probably because I had worked for Mr. Kirk for a number of years at his mine in Goodsprings, Nevada, which National Lead Company had purchased.

Leah: What happened then?

Earl: I got busy at Stampede working like the dickens with whatever men I could get to extract the ore.

Leah: Was there a problem keeping people working at the mine?

Earl: No not really. I could always find help. The first winter when we started mining over there we had no compressor or rock drills. All we had was what little planes couldn't bring in. All the work was with 'single-jack' and I had no problem finding men in town that still knew how to swing a hammer. Earlier I had two brothers working for me out at Chatham Creek where we were doing some prospecting. I hired them, and when I got authority from National Lead, I hired Bill Taylor (he owned the mining claim before I took it over) to go to Lignite and build a winter sled road from Lignite into Stampede. He knew the country and was the best man for the job. If I had hired some engineers to survey and do all that, Bill would have had to be along anyway to guide them, and Bill could build the road and pick up what men he needed; I didn't have to worry about it. I just flew in with Lon Brennen who was a pilot. We landed as close as we could. First we dropped our ham, bacon and perishables from the plane. We had a clear place on the river, two miles from where we were mining. We had to land down about six or seven miles. We broke the tail skid off the plane. Lon said that it would be two days before he could come back. When we left town, I hadn't brought my old dog, Kobuk. We couldn't get him in the plane with all of the freight, and Lon was going to bring him back the next day. Another thing that was a worry was that I had no guns, and I was walking up and down, six miles to the camp with that first load, then back down to get the ham, bacon and perishables, and then one more round trip to get my sleeping bag and clothes. The cabin had no windows in it, just one log on each side cut out about six inches wide for a window. The door had hinges made of wood and quick-sawed boards for a door. Up the trail toward the mine there was a wheelbarrow made all out of wood, even a wooden wheel.

Jim: It would be nice to have preserved that.

Earl: I wish I had done that.

Jim: It was pretty unique.

Earl: It was some time before we brought in a metal wheelbarrow ourselves. You don't think of some of those things.

Jim: The craftsmen they had in those days...it's just a dying art. It's gone.

Earl: If you wanted to make one out of wood like that, I could give you a representative drawing of what it looked like. That old one laid around and fell apart. I should have preserved it. I never asked Bill if he made that wheelbarrow. As I said, he owned the claim before me.

Jim: Wasn't Bill Taylor the first man to climb Mount McKinley?

Earl: Him and his partner were. They didn't climb the real mountain. They thought the one closest to Fairbanks was the highest. Actually, it's 2 or 300 feet shorter. They had brought a flagpole with them. They climbed with this 14-foot pole and some coil wire to stake it up there. They hoisted it with a flag attached on it. They packed that all the way up.

Jim: Did they get credit for being the first ones to climb McKinley?

Earl: No they didn't. A kind of influential man forced his way into their group. He wasn't an athletic man, they had to leave him at the 3,000-foot level in this cave with whiskey. He stayed at the 3,000-foot level waiting for them. After they came down, he went to Fairbanks and told them he'd climbed McKinley. People believed him because he was influential, even though, at first, they didn't think it was possible because many experienced mountain climbers who had come from other parts of the world had failed.

Jim: Somebody asked Taylor what he took for grub the last day of the climb. Tell Leah that story.

Earl: One morning when Bill and I were taking these two men from National Lead to examine Stampede, Bill was preparing breakfast, and this director of the big mining company says, "Now Bill, on that last day that you climbed, what did you take for your food?" Bill was stirring some bacon or something in a frying pan. Bill says, "Two doughnuts." We all just roared in laughter.

Jim: Can you imagine, two doughnuts for your last day? Awful optimistic.

Earl: Bill himself was quite a character.

Jim: I bet he was.

Earl: He was built about like you—husky build. I knew him very well.

Jim: Did he ask you one time to go up to Mount McKinley with him, or was that someone else?

Earl: Oh that was the chief ranger of McKinley Park. When they came to the Stampede we put them up and fed them and got along pretty good with them. Those people in McKinley were National Park Rangers. They get their orders directly from Washington (D.C.). Most of these people have never been to Alaska before and don't know what to do. As soon as the park expanded and took in Stampede, they broke into my log-cabin office. Except for that original one, I built all of the other buildings, seven or eight cabins. When I closed up that first year, I expected I'd be there for a long time because these new people who bought it would come in, operate the mine, sink a shaft and do diamond drilling. The diamond drilling machinery is all in there now, everything is there and ready to go. I didn't know that they bought the mine solely as a tax write-off.

Leah: Is there any mining going on there now?

Earl: None. Mr. Beistline took some students in there to work on something. A year or two before that, a Canadian professor—a Canadian Indian prince—was in there with some students, checking on the warehouse, equipment. That's about all.

Jim: When you were working the mine at Stampede, what was the biggest crew that you had. I know you have a pretty large bunkhouse over there.

Earl: I had a dozen, counting the cook. As far as I know, it was the second largest antimony-producing mine in North America, and there's lots of ore left, and I don't want it tied up in perpetuity. Is that how it's pronounced?

Leah: Is that in the (Denali National) Park boundary?

Jim: Yeah. I don't know what the status is.

Earl: If the National Park Service had its way, they'd lock it up tight. Then it would be unusable.

Jim: You have an airfield there. The ore could be flown out.

Earl: My airport was outside the park boundary, and the mine was not inside the park. If they hadn't deliberately put it in during this d-2 bill, I could be working it today if the market price was high enough. I shut down when the market was low, of course. I had closed the mine down, and had started to make the changes to add some more equipment to the mill, and then this "wonderful gentleman" wrote me a letter, that wanted to buy the mine.

Jim: What time of the year was that?

Earl: December, and I wrote back that it wasn't a good time of year to examine a mine, and that he should wait until summer to send his geologist or engineer in. I welcomed him and his geologist in to examine the mine.

Jim: Did you ever get a copy of his evaluation and report ?

Earl: No, I never did.

Jim: Did you ask for it?

Earl: Oh yeah I did.

Jim: They never did give it to you?

Earl: Well, it didn't matter anyway. If the report was favorable, and I knew the mine was favorable, but I figured this man would give a phony report, but they went ahead with their option. They came in the next year in the middle of winter, same way. We made a deal, but they didn't intend to go through with it. This d-2 election was voted on, and it was right down their alley. It put us in the park, and that beautiful, handsome President Carter there signed it. This guy knew what was happening and simply wanted a tax write-off.

Jim: Could it be reopened now?

Earl: Now if a war should start and we needed antimony in a hurry, the military would have to convince Congress that they should allow the Stampede to reopen. With the Park Service headquarters right in the middle of it. Impossible!

Jim: We don't want to get Earl's dander up talking about this kind of stuff. It's not good for your blood pressure, Earl. Although the last time Earl went out for a physical, the doctor told him that he would probably live to be over 100 or at least 100. Earl was disappointed, because he had planned to live to 120. He was disappointed in the doctor's statement. Do you have anything else you would like to say, Earl?

Earl: I've told this young lady too much already. Let's go to lunch.

Jim: Before we quit I want to tell Leah that two of Earl's ex-wives are still alive and they both love him.

Part V

Where
The Trail Winds

Where The Trail Winds

Following the interviews, contributors and I have stayed in touch. The following summaries provide the reader with a brief history of these contributing pioneers over the most recent years.

Johne Binkley

Johne lives in Fairbanks, where he serves as president and CEO of Alaska Riverways, the family business originally started by his father and mother, Captain Jim and Mary Binkley. He also serves as president of the El Dorado Gold Mine, a Binkley Family enterprise that offers visitors an opportunity to experience Alaska's gold mining history. A few of Johne's community service efforts include serving as chairman of the board of directors on the Alaska Railroad Corporation, serving on the board of directors of ENSTAR Natural Gas and on the Alaska Airlines advisory board. Johne's personal interests include flying, working with youth hockey and membership in the Alaska Trapper's Association.

Terrence Cole

Terrence is still a history professor at the University of Alaska Fairbanks, and is also Director of the Office of Public History in the UAF Rasmuson Library. He continues to pursue his studies on Alaskan history. His most recent work is a monograph on the economic history of Alaska's petroleum industry entitled, "Blended by Riches."

Shann Jones

Shann continues to live in Fairbanks with his wife, Teresa, and son, Devin. Shann works for the University of Alaska Fairbanks Geophysical Institute Operations Office as a program assistant. In addition he is an instructor of Outdoor Activities at the University of Alaska Fairbanks' Tanana Valley Campus Recreation Program where he specializes in adult outdoor recreation program development and delivery. One of Shann's more interesting duties is taking bi-weekly absolute measurements of the Earth's magnetic field for the U. S. Geological Survey.

Jim Lounsbury

Jim continues to call Fairbanks his home, but works as an equipment operator and foreman of the State of Alaska Department of Transportation Road Maintenance at Coldfoot, Alaska. In the summer he spends much of his spare time in Wiseman, 15 miles north of Coldfoot, where he and his wife, Lorna, run a history related business called the Wiseman Gold Rush Camp Bed and Breakfast. Jim's public service interest is youth hockey. He is heavily involved in setting up the outdoor hockey and skating rink in Fairbanks, where young people can learn to skate and enjoy the sport of hockey. His hobby is antique cars. He is a member of the local antique car club where he enjoys showing his 1926 Dodge—a vehicle he personally restored from the ground up.

Leah Madonna

Leah still lives in Fairbanks where she continues to run her prospecting and mining equipment store, Alaskan Prospectors. In the summer she is also active in gardening, and during the winter she enjoys writing short stories. During the winter months she also enjoys traveling to the Tucson Gem and Mineral Show and Quartzite, where she purchases minerals for the store and to fill customer requests. When asked what her plans are for the near future she replied, "I plan to continue running the store, on a limited basis, and will be traveling to the Brooks Range this summer where I will spend some time at Del and Gail Ackels mining camp and do some metal detecting and prospecting."

Felix Pedro

Felix died on July 22, 1910, at the age of 52, exactly eight years after his discovery of gold on Pedro Creek. On October 12, 1972, following years of unrest and obscurity, his remains were respectfully laid to rest in the cemetery located in the land where he was born—Fanano, Italy. Felix is as restless following death as he was during life. In 2005, just as this book was going to press, it was learned through communications with Massimo Turchi that Felix's body has been exhumed and subjected to modern forensic investigations to determine if indeed there was any evidence to support the allegation that he was murdered by the insertion of a needle into the back of his head and to determine if the body is truly that of Felix Pedro. The results of the investigation indicated that there was no evidence to support the needle fable and the remains were indeed that of Felix Pedro. The story doesn't end: according to Massimo, there was some discussion regarding moving Felix's remains a short distance from Fanano to the village of Trignano, where he was born. Later, that suggestion was overruled and Felix's remains were returned to the vault in the Fanano cemetery. It can be concluded that the history of Felix's adventurous life is mirrored in his restlessness since death. In life and in death he truly has one of the most colorful and adventurous histories of mankind. Perhaps now he can rest in peace—time will tell.

Earl Pilgrim

Earl died at the Pioneers Home in Fairbanks, Alaska on August 26, 1987 at the age of 94. He was cremated in Fairbanks and Jim Lounsbury and his brother George Lounsbury spread his ashes around his cabin at the Stampede Mine near Mt. McKinley.

Massimo Turchi

Massimo still lives in Fanano, Modena, Italy, where he is in charge of tourism and developing new tourism activities. He works mostly with North European markets in developing hiking and cycling tours. He also manages the two visitor centers of the Frignano Natural and Regional Park in the high Appanine Mountains of Modena. Massimo's public service activities include working with local schools on historical and environmental themes.

Part VI

Appendices
and
Suggested Reading

Appendix I
Alaska Facts

Appendix II
Alaska Gold Discoveries

Appendix III
Suggested Reading
and
Alaska Pioneers Featured in Volumes I, II and III

Appendix I

Alaska Facts

Alaska Highway: Begins at Dawson Creek, British Columbia (mile 0) and runs 1,520 miles to Fairbanks, Alaska. Prior to its construction in 1942, travel to Alaska was primarily by water.

Arctic Circle: Approximately 66°30' north from the equator. Also is the latitude at which the sun does not set during the summer solstice (June 20 or 21) or rise during the winter solstice (December 21 or 22).

Aurora Borealis: Commonly known as Northern Lights are light displays in the northern hemisphere that occur in response to charged particles entering the Earth's atmosphere. The result of these charged particles striking gas particles is the creation of light displays which are often observed as variably colored movement of serpent type arcs and draperies in the Alaskan skies.

Alaska Bush: areas of wilderness outside the major population areas; includes numerous small towns and villages.

Cabin Fever: A state of discontent produced when a person is snowbound in a small cabin or room.

Cheechako: A newcomer or greenhorn that has recently just arrived in Alaska.

State Capital: Juneau.

Population (1998): 607,800

Size: The largest state; approximately one fifth the size of the conterminous 48 states, with an area of 570,374 square miles (365,000,000 acres).

Coastline: 6,640 miles.

State Bird: Willow Ptarmigan.

State Fish: King Salmon.

State Flower: Forget-Me-Not.

State Fossil: Woolly Mammoth.

State Gem: Jade.

State Insect: Four-Spot Skimmer Dragonfly.

State Marine Mammal: Bowhead Whale.

State Mineral: Gold.

State Motto: North to the Future.

State Sport: Dog Mushing.

State Tree: Sitka Spruce.

Appendix II

Alaska Gold Discoveries

1862-Placer gold discovered on the Stikine River.

1870-Placer gold found at Sumdum Bay, Southeastern Alaska.

1871-Placer gold found near Wrangell, Southeastern Alaska

1872-Gold in quartz found near Sitka (Stewart Mine).

1875-Placer gold found on Shuck River, Windham Bay, Southeastern Alaska.

1880-Joseph Juneau and Richard T. Harris, discover placer and lode gold at Juneau.

1884-Lode gold found at Unga Island in Southwestern Alaska.

1886-Lode gold discovered at Berners Bay, Southeastern Alaska.

1886-Howard Franklin discovers placer gold on Fortymile River and on Franklin Creek.

1887-Placer gold found on beaches of Yakutat and Lituya Bays.

1888-Placer gold found on Resurrection Creek, Kenai Peninsula.

1893-Pitka and Sorresco discover placer gold on Birch Creek (Circle District).

1896-Placer gold found in the Klondike District, Yukon Territory, independently by Robert Henderson and George W. Carmack.

1897-Placer gold found on Ophir Creek, Seward Peninsula.

1898-Klondike Stampede.

1898-Placer gold found in Porcupine District near Haines.

1898-Placer gold found at Nome by Jafet Lindenberg, Jon Bryantson and Eric O. Lindblom.

1899-Placer gold discovered on Upper Koyukuk River.

1899-Nome beach gold discovered.

1902-Placer gold found in the Tanana District (Fairbanks) by Felix Pedro.

1903-Placer gold found in the Bonnifield District.

1903-Placer gold found at Denali (Valdez Creek) on upper Susitna River.

1905-Placer gold found in the Kantishna District.

1906-Placer gold found in Tenderfoot District.

1906-Placer and quartz gold found in Chandalar District by Frank Yasuda and Thomas G. Carter, partners.

1906-Gold in quartz found in Willow District.

1906-Placer gold found on Games Creek, Innoko District.

1907-Placer gold found in Talkeetna (Yentna) District.

1907-Placer gold found in Ruby District.

1907-Gold discovered on Nolan Creek, Upper Koyukuk District.

1909-Placer gold discovered in Iditarod District by John Benton and W.A. Dikeman.

1909-Placer gold discovered on Klery Creek, Kiana, Kobuk District.

1910-Placer gold discovered near Hughes, middle Koyukuk.

1900-1914-Lower Kuskokwim, Arolik River and Wattamus Creek stampeds.

1911-Placer gold found on Hammond River, Upper Koyukuk. First copper shipped from Kennicott.

1912-Placer gold discovered at Chisana (Shushana).

1913-Placer gold discovered at Nelchina.

1913-Placer gold discovered at Marshall, lower Yukon.

1914-Placer gold found at Tolavana District (Livengood).

1924-Large scale dredging program at Fairbanks planned.

1926-Placer platinum discovered at Goodnews Bay: small scale mining until 1934 when mining with mechanical equipment began.

1942-Gold mining prohibited by law because of war.

1945-Gold mining again allowed by law.

1970-I.L. Tailleur recognizes potential Red Dog deposit.

1972-Record low gold production of only 8,639 ounces statewide.

1973-O'Dea vein at Grant Mine property discovered by Roger Burggraf and Gilbert Dobbs.

1974-Private ownership of gold permitted.

1974-1983-Rise in gold prices to $850 per ounce stimulates gold rush to Alaska.

1977-Greens Creek silver, lead-zinc prospect near Juneau discovered.

1981-Gold production jumps to 134,200 ounces nearly doubling previous year's total.

1983-Joe Taylor Jr. discovers hardrock gold in the Cleary Summit area near Fairbanks which leads to development of the Fort Knox project.

1985-Underground hardrock ore production begun at the Grant Mine near Fairbanks in October.

1987-"Bima" dredge begins offshore placer mining near Nome June 16.

1987-Surface hardrock ore production begun at the Grant Mine near Fairbanks in October.

1987-Citigold Alaska heap leaches first gold from Ryan lode near Fairbanks.

1989-Greens Creek hard rock silver, lead-zinc mine near Juneau goes into operation.

1990-Red Dog lead-zinc mine near Kotzebue opens.

1991-Cambior Alaska reopens Valdez Creek placer gold mine near Cantwell.

1993-Greens Creek Mine near Juneau closes in April because of low metal prices.

1995-Valdez Creek placer mine near Cantwell closes.

1995-Sumitomo announces gold discovery at Pogo prospect near Delta Junction.

1995-Nixon Fork hard rock gold-copper mine near McGrath goes into production in October.

1996-Greens Creek Mine near Juneau reopens.

1996-Fort Knox hard rock gold mine near Fairbanks goes into production in November.

Appendix III

Suggested Reading

Alaska-Yukon Magazine, "Felix Pedro." 1909, volume 7, #4.

Borchard, Heinz (translation from Italian). "Felix Pedro: A mystery man who struck it rich." Fairbanks, Daily News-Miner, July 21, 1989.

Cashen, William R. Farthest North College President. University of Alaska Press, Fairbanks, Alaska, 1972.

Cohen, Stan. The Trail of 42 - A Pictorial History of the Alaska Highway, Altona, Manitoba, Canada Friesen Printers, 1979.

Cole, Dermot. "Family ties to Felix Pedro cover a lot of miles." Fairbanks Daily News-Miner, September 1, 1999.

Cole, Terrence. Crooked Past: The History of a Frontier Mining Camp: Fairbanks Alaska. University of Alaska Press, 1991.

Cole, Terrence. Nome—"City of the Golden Beaches." Alaska Geographic, Vol. 11, Number 1.

DeArmond, Robert. "This Month In Northland History: Fairbanks, July 25, 1910." Alaska Sportsman, July 1968.

Fairbanks Evening News, To Italy For Bride. Tuesday, July 18, 1905.

Heller, Herbert L. Sourdough Sagas. Cleveland, Ohio, The New World Publishing Company 1967,

"Ingrid Martin, Prospector's descendant digs his golden roots" (Interview with Philip Lelli). Fairbanks Daily News Miner, July 18, 1990.

Mullen, Donna Salter. Felix Pedro: His Fame and His Pedroni Family. Privately produced manuscript, 2002.

Oehring, Connie. "Felix Pedro Monument Rededicated." Fairbanks Daily News-Miner, July 23, 1986.

Ogilvie, William. Early Days on the Yukon. London and New York: J. Lane, 1913.

Parker, Genevieve Alice. "The Evolution of Placer Mining Methods in Alaska." B.S. Thesis, Alaska Agricultural College and School of Mines, 1929.

Patty, Stanton H. Felix Pedro—A Mystery." Alaska Journal, Autumn, 1971, Vol.1, #4.

Patty, Stanton H. "The Restless Remains of Felix Pedro." Seattle Times, May 21, 1972.

Pedro, Mary Ellen v. Pedro, Felix. Court Document 26221. Superior Court of the State of Washington, November, 1908.

Pellegrini, Angelo. "The Felix (Pedro) Pedroni Story." V.F. Hall Manuscript a translation from Italian, June 15, 1952. University of Alaska Fairbanks Archives.

"Quinn's Story Of Discovery On Pedro Creek. Fairbanks, Alaska" Jessen's Weekly, Thursday, July 17, 1953, Vol. 1, Number 29.

Spring, Abe. "Early History of the Tanana Valley." Alaska-Yukon Magazine 1909, Vol 7, #4.

"The Fairbanks Mines, Nome And Dawson Rivalled, Discovery And Value." Fairbanks Miner, Fairbanks, Alaska, May, 1903, (University of Alaska Archives).

Turchi, Massimo. Felice Pedroni & Felix Pedro, From Trignano to Fairbanks, The Journey of A Fanano Emigrant. Municipality of Fanano, edited by "Debatte Otello srl," September 2003.

Wharton, David. The Alaska Gold Rush Bloomington, Indiana, Indiana University Press, 1972.

Wickersham, James. Old Yukon: Tales-Trails-and Trials. Washington Law Book Co.: Washington, D. C., 1938.

Life in Alaska's Frontier as Told by the Pioneers who Blazed the Trails

Pioneers Featured in Volume I

Jim Binkley	Don Nelson
Mary Binkley	Jeannette Therriault
Doug Colp	Hector Therriault
Robert Charlie	Rudy Vetter
Tony Gularte	Doris Vogler
Cliff Haydon	Joe Vogler
Orea Haydon	Ernie Wolff
Juanita Helms	William Wood
Duke Kilbury	Shorty Zucchini
Don May	Paul McCarthy

Pioneers Featured in Volume II

Del Ackels	Harold Gillam
Gail Ackles	Mary Hansen
Steve Agbaba	Roy Larson
Paul Barelka	Enid Magill
Bill Boucher	Fred Magill
Frieda Chamberlain	Irene Mead
Emery Chapple	Cy Randell
Don Cook	Hazel Randell
Bette Fahrenkamp	Stu Rothman
Mack Fenton	Leon Tromley

Pioneers Featured in Volume III

Ed Ashby	Maurice "Ozzie" Oswald
Jim Bell	Tim Sander
Bob Cowgill	Mary Shields
Janet Cowgill	Tom Snapp
Bob Hamilton	Sandra Stillion
Jerry Hassel	Oden Stranberg
Phil Holdsworth	Mary Lou Teel
Bob Jacobs	Helen Warner
Neville Jacobs	Arnold "Swede" Wasvick
Ray Lester	Nedra Waterman
Leah Madonna	Wes Waterman
John Miscovich	Jack Williams

$14.95 Each
www.alaskagoldinformationcenter.com

504 College Rd.
Fairbanks, Alaska 99701

National Award Winning Videos
by
Jim Madonna

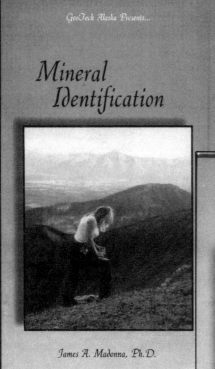

GeoTech Alaska Presents...

Mineral Identification

James A. Madonna, Ph.D.

The Art of
Mineral Identification
103 minutes
$39.95 includes shipping

GeoTech Alaska Presents...

The Art of

Gold Identification

James A. Madonna, Ph.D.

The Art of
Gold Identification
34 minutes
$19.95 includes shipping

Products of GeoTech Alaska
504 College Rd,
Fairbanks, Alaska 99701
907-452-7398
www.alaskagoldinformationcenter.com